D0945258

The Historic Kentucky Kitchen

The Historic Kentucky Kitchen

Traditional Recipes for Today's Cook

Deirdre A. Scaggs
and
Andrew W. McGraw

Foreword by
John van Willigen

UNIVERSITY PRESS OF KENTUCKY

Scholarly publisher for the Commonwealth,
serving Bellarmine University, Berea College, Centre College of Kentucky,
Eastern Kentucky University, The Filson Historical Society, Georgetown
College, Kentucky Historical Society, Kentucky State University, Morehead
State University, Murray State University, Northern Kentucky University,
Transylvania University, University of Kentucky, University of Louisville,
and Western Kentucky University.
All rights reserved.

Editorial and Sales Offices: The University Press of Kentucky
663 South Limestone Street, Lexington, Kentucky 40508-4008
www.kentuckypress.com

Frontispiece: Long table setting, August 16, 1918. Louis Edward Nollau F
Series Photographic Print Collection, University of Kentucky Libraries.

17 16 15 14 13   5 4 3 2 1

Library of Congress Cataloging-in-Publication Data

Scaggs, Deirdre A.
  The historic Kentucky kitchen : traditional recipes for today's cook / Deirdre
A. Scaggs and Andrew W. McGraw ; foreword by John van Willigen.
    pages cm
  Includes bibliographical references and index.
  ISBN 978-0-8131-4249-4 (hardcover : alkaline paper) —
  ISBN 978-0-8131-4303-3 (epub) — ISBN 978-0-8131-4304-0 (pdf)
  1. Cooking, American—Southern style. 2. Cooking—Kentucky.
  3. Cooking—Kentucky—History. I. McGraw, Andrew W., 1978- II. Title.
  TX715.2.S68S29 2013
  641.5975—dc23   2013018946

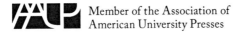

For the egg sandwich expert, Roger Scaggs;

Dorothy Wilson and her cast-iron skillet;

and

Jane Gore

Contents

Foreword

Recipes

Cookbooks and their recipes are important and historically revealing, because in addition to techniques of food preparation, they give us an understanding of people's lives. While published cookbooks are important, manuscript recipes are another aspect of foodways. Almost every cook has a collection of recipes, often handwritten or typed, in a file folder or a shoe box. In *The Historic Kentucky Kitchen: Traditional Recipes for Today's Cook,* University of Kentucky archivist Deirdre Scaggs helps us experience the domain of recipes beyond published cookbooks. Deirdre draws on her extensive experience working with historic Kentucky archival materials and her well-developed skills in cooking and recipe testing to compile a unique account of an important, but little-known, aspect of Kentucky foodways, manuscript recipes. She makes Kentucky culinary history clearer by providing a glimpse of some important manuscript recipe collections in archives at the University of Kentucky. To help provide a context for this cookbook, let us look at the history of cookbooks in Kentucky.

In the overall scheme of things, cookbooks are relatively new. The first European settlements in Kentucky date from 1774, yet the earliest Kentucky cookbook was not published until 1839. *The Kentucky Housewife,* written by Boyle County native Lettice

Bryan, is still celebrated as one of the foundation texts of southern cooking. Certainly there were cookbooks in use prior to this classic, but they probably came from either England or New England. The point is that for a long time cooking was done without benefit of published cookbooks or even written recipes. Based on my own excursions in the kitchen, it is probably true that most cooking still doesn't involve written recipes, in cookbooks or not. After a while we go beyond the recipes, and as Kentucky cookbook author Marion W. Flexner wrote, we "cook by ear." I recall my astonishment, after sitting down for a Sunday dinner at a couple's home in rural Kentucky, at learning that my hostess had made such delicious biscuits without a recipe. With experience, we come to understand how cooking works and use that knowledge to cook. In between the cookbook and "cooking by ear" is the manuscript recipe.

Cookbooks published from historic manuscript recipe collections are rare. Easily the most celebrated manuscript cookbook in the American culinary tradition is the one that came to be published as *Martha Washington's Booke of Cookery,* edited by well-known culinary historian Karen Hess. This collection of recipes was in the possession of our first First Lady starting in 1749. Mrs. Washington passed it on to her granddaughter Eleanor Parke Custis. Like most published cookbooks that started as manuscript cookbooks, it is hard to date and just a little mysterious. There are lots of mystery ingredients and novel recipes. The editor and annotator, Karen Hess, appropriately called the recipes beguiling. A more recent cookbook of this type, one far more attuned to Kentucky, is *The John Jacob Niles Cook Book.* This little volume, published in 1996 by a small Lexington publisher, began as the files and notes of the man who is central Kentucky's contribution to American folk music. It was put together from Niles's notebooks and files by Mary Rannells after his death.

Manuscript recipes have certain characteristics. First, handwritten recipes are fast, while cookbooks are slow. How often have you said, "Can you give me that recipe?" after eating a memorable dish? Similarly fast are clipped recipes. Frequently one can see clipped recipes in community cookbooks. These often have ingredients listed by brand names. Many cookbooks include space for recipes to be written or pasted in. A most interesting sidebar to collecting old cookbooks is the recipes written in them and the clipped recipes on old newsprint found browning among the pages. These clipped-out or handwritten recipes often are the foundation for the writing of new cookbooks in that they often reflect the new and the novel for the cooks involved.

Manuscript recipe books allow sharing between friends and neighbors. Swapped recipes are something like social media. Including a person's recipe in one's collection is a little like friending someone on Facebook. Giving a recipe a place serves to link us together, solidifies a shared memory, and provides us with an affiliation. Of course, the practice is useful for cooking, too. This works in both social time and social space. The intriguing question is what people are represented in the selection of a recipe. A quick review of community cookbooks shows that people have tended to contribute recipes from loved ones, famous food writers, other famous persons, or famous restaurants. Think Mom's stack cake, Cissy Gregg's dumplings, Beaumont Inn's corn pudding.

Handwritten recipes can have special meanings. I still bake cookies from a recipe card in the handwriting of my mother, who died years ago. It's a recipe for what was always called Dutch pretzels in the family. Lots of family lore is attached to the recipe, which I assume was from my Dutch grandmother. My father in his retirement used to get involved in the preparation. The unbaked cookies are coated with cinnamon and sugar, and he wanted to make sure that the cookies had lots of sugar on them because he liked the crunch. There is something very comfortable about reading my mother's instructions in her clear and reassuring script; placing the index card carefully on top of its oak recipe file while mixing, forming, and baking the cookies; and then, when the job is done, placing the card back in the file under "Cookies," near the recipe for snickerdoodles that my wife, Jackie, made for our daughters. With the comfort comes tension, though, as I worry about losing the recipe card. The point is that handwritten recipes can be a link with the past.

Manuscript recipes are usually simpler than published recipes, and sometimes they are little more than a list of ingredients and their measures. Perhaps that's because the kind of person who would bother writing down someone else's recipe would know how to cook and would not need to have cooking instructions added to the recipe. Contemporary Kentucky cookbooks, especially those written by single authors, tend to include detailed discussions of procedures. Manuscript recipes are written just to be cooked and eaten. However, in contemporary Kentucky cookbooks, we can find narratives that take us beyond the ingredient list and other instructions to very interesting discussions of the history of the recipe, the place where the food was eaten, the history of the community, and many other topics. Early appearances of such well-developed narratives in Kentucky cookbooks can be found in the 1940s cookbooks of Marion W. Flexner and in the limited culinary writing of humorist Tandy Ellis in the 1920s. Robust narratives also appear in some community cookbooks, such as the many published by the Magoffin County Historical Society.

Deirdre Scaggs has provided an exploration of some important Kentucky manuscript recipe collections ranging from around the 1870s to the 1960s and from hearth cooking to cooking on more or less modern gas or electric stoves. We can hold these recipes in our hands and share a link with the historic past. And thanks to the author's considerable cooking skills, the recipes are made usable in our kitchens.

Nothing is better than a good read followed by good eats.

John van Willigen,
Professor Emeritus of Anthropology,
University of Kentucky
Author of *Food and Everyday Life
on Kentucky Family Farms,
1920–1950* and other books

Preface

The idea for this book arose from a small recipe and a lot of curiosity. While processing the Logan English papers, held by the University of Kentucky Libraries Special Collections, Andrew McGraw and I pulled a box to get a general sense of what was in the collection. Inside an arbitrary folder from a randomly chosen archival box, we found our first recipe. It had no title but proved to be a delicious combination of zucchini, tomatoes, anchovy, and eggs. This defining moment was followed by a question. Why not compile a cookbook of Kentucky recipes from the archives? We knew there had to be more, and we set off to find them. Our mouths watered at the recipes we found, and we were struck not only by the number of collections containing recipes, but also by the way these recipes were spread out across the history of Kentucky. Finding the recipes was just part of the process. Cooking them was the lure. When we began cooking, the creation of *The Historic Kentucky Kitchen: Traditional Recipes for Today's Cook* began.

Introduction

This book is a collection of nineteenth- and twentieth-century recipes from the University of Kentucky Libraries Special Collections. Archival collections were scoured for clues that would lead us to finding recipes: journals, scrapbooks, and books of "receipts"—an old term for "recipe." Most of the recipes included in this book are adapted from handwritten recipes in the archives, many are from clippings pasted in scrapbooks, and some are from historic Kentucky cookbooks. We thought it was important to focus on the handwritten recipes; they seemed more cherished, more likely to have been used to prepare food in Kentucky homes, and more traditional or authentic to Kentucky's food history. We hope we are giving these rediscovered historic recipes new life and the chance to be passed down to future generations.

Because the two of us share a passion for food and Kentucky history, there was a natural connection that led to creating a historical cookbook. One thing that sets this cookbook apart from others is that all of the recipes included have been tested, and many of them retested. With few exceptions, the recipes are not modified to alter the taste or core values of the dish. Whenever possible we obtained the ingredients locally. Most recipe modifications were substitutions for a fat or for a rare or extinct ingredient, and these substitutions are indicated throughout the book. The most significant addition is that we supplied notes on preparation, cooking times, and oven temperature, because few of the early originals contained these procedures. Although we want to convey a sense of the original cooking environment, we've done everything possible to make the recipes user-friendly for modern home cooks.

These recipes were hand-selected based on their timelessness and our personal tastes, to represent the culinary diversity of the area and fulfill our desire to preserve Kentucky history through regional recipes. Our Kentucky heritage is unique, and we want to celebrate and preserve it by sharing recipes from the collective memories of our elders. These recipes carry the aura of a different time and a slower pace of life, in which meals were handmade and shared. It is this ritual, by means of these recipes, that we hope to preserve.

Most of these early American cooks (or collectors) preserved their recipes in handwritten volumes, and few of them have been published. Here you will see a mixture of African, English, French, American, and southern flavors. Perhaps the desire to create this cookbook comes from our inborn southern drive for hospitality—to serve and share good food with family, friends, and even strangers. In any case, this cookbook will help to keep the durable southern tradition alive with recipes from our collective history.

When a person's name appears in a recipe title, it is the individual who compiled or collected the recipe. Some dishes may be credited to another, but like the recipes in your kitchen, they may have been handed down from family or friends, clipped from a newspaper, or shared by neighbors. These are titled only to show who *collected* them, not to indicate who made them distinctive, local, or even southern.

Since many of these handwritten recipes did not use standardized measurements, the following will help if you should decide to try cooking your own dishes from historic texts.

Two women and a man preparing food for a surveying class, circa 1930s–1940s. Louis Edward Nollau F Series Photographic Print Collection, University of Kentucky Libraries.

Measurements

A pinch or dash	roughly ⅛ teaspoon
1 kitchen spoon	1 teaspoon
1 dessert or soup spoon	2 teaspoons
1 spoonful	1 tablespoon
Butter the size of a walnut	roughly 2 tablespoons
Butter the size of a hen's egg	3 to 4 tablespoons
1 pound of flour	approximately 4 cups
1 pound of sugar	approximately 2 cups
1 pound of eggs	8 with their shells, 10 without
1 gill	4 fluid ounces or ½ cup
1 teacup	6 fluid ounces or ¾ cup
1 wine glass	2 fluid ounces or ¼ cup

1 tumbler	8 fluid ounces or 1 cup
1 coffee cup	nearly 8 fluid ounces

Milk Substitutions

Sweet milk	milk that has not soured; use whole milk
Sweet cream	use heavy cream
Sour milk	milk that has soured; while buttermilk is not quite the same, it can be used. Or sour whole milk by adding 1 tablespoon of lemon juice per cup of milk.
Milk	Whole milk

Oven Temperatures (Fahrenheit)

Slow	300 degrees
Moderate	350 degrees
Quick	375 to 400 degrees
Hot	400 to 425 degrees

Preserving eggs, circa 1940s. Louis Edward Nollau Nitrate Photographic Print Collection, University of Kentucky Libraries.

Egg and Cheese Dishes

The southern breakfast is symbolic of much that is distinctive and exemplary about food in the South.
—*John Egerton*, Southern Food in History

Because cows and chickens were abundant on southern farms, egg, milk, and cheese dishes were enjoyed often at the southern table. Most of the dishes in this chapter are breakfast fare, but the tasty combination also shows up in casseroles, soufflés, and sauces throughout southern contemporary and historical cuisine. No one has ruled that an omelet is good only at breakfast, and most certainly the other dishes can be served as main dishes, sides, or desserts. The tomato fricassee was an absolute delight. Although a fricassee is normally made with meat, and typically chicken, this rich gravy has been popular since the colonial era.

Frances Jewell McVey's Meat Soufflé, circa 1920s

This dish is light and fluffy. Because the roux is so thick, the meat is distributed evenly throughout the soufflé. We used one-half pound of Kentucky ground bison breakfast sausage, but any ground meat would be good. Please note that ground meats such as turkey or chicken would require extra salt.[1]

6 to 8 servings

1 cup ground cooked meat
3 eggs, separated
3 tablespoons butter
3 tablespoons flour
2 tablespoons diced onion
1 teaspoon salt
⅛ teaspoon paprika
½ cup milk

Preheat the oven to 350 degrees. Brown the meat in an oven-proof skillet over medium heat. Set the meat aside and discard the pan drippings. Beat the egg yolks in a separate bowl. Using an electric or hand mixer, whip the whites until they stand in soft peaks. In the same skillet, over medium to medium-low heat, melt the butter and add the flour. Stir until this mixture is slightly browned; add the onion, salt, and paprika. Stir to combine. Gradually add the milk and cook until smooth and thick, stirring frequently. Add the meat along with the beaten egg yolks and stir until combined. Remove the mixture from the heat and fold in the beaten egg whites gradually. Bake for 30 minutes or until firm and lightly browned. Loosen the edges with a spatula before serving.

Cheese Soufflé

Delightfully light and exceptionally creamy, this circa 1920s soufflé would make a nice, sweet accompaniment for brunch; it could even serve as a light dessert. This dish is a highly recommended treat that will surprise and impress guests. Once prepared, serve it immediately.[2]

4 servings

¼ cup sour cream
8 ounces Neufchâtel cheese
5 tablespoons honey
3 eggs
¼ teaspoon salt

Preheat the oven to 350 degrees. Heat the sour cream and cheese over low heat stirring until very smooth. Remove the cheese mixture from the heat, add the honey, and mix well. Separate the egg yolks from the whites. Mix the salt into the yolks in a small bowl and set aside. Using an electric or hand mixer, whip the egg whites until they are stiff but not dry. Add the yolks to the cheese and mix to combine. Fold in one-fourth of the egg whites at first to lighten the cheese and egg mixture; then gently fold in the rest. Fill four individual pastry cases or custard cups and bake for 25 minutes.

Scrambled Eggs with Cottage Cheese

These scrambled eggs are as creamy as French omelets: soft, flavorful, and melting in your mouth. The eggs would be terrific served over an English muffin or toast. Allot two eggs per person and adjust the amounts accordingly. The original recipe reads, "Neutralize the acid in the cheese with soda and stir into the egg, serve immediately." It did not seem to affect the flavor of the dish, but we followed the instructions faithfully.[3]

2 servings

4 eggs
½ teaspoon salt or more to taste
Pepper to taste
4 tablespoons milk
½ teaspoon baking soda
4 rounded tablespoons cottage cheese

Mix the eggs, salt, pepper, and milk. Scramble the mixture in a greased skillet over medium heat. Remove from heat, sprinkle the baking soda over the cottage cheese, and stir into the egg mixture. Serve immediately.

Frances Jewell McVey's Tomatoes with Eggs, circa 1920s

An interesting recipe from the early to mid twentieth century. Fresh summer tomatoes are the key to making this a moist, flavorful dish. Don't cook the eggs too long, or they will become hard; they will continue to cook briefly after being removed from the oven. The original recipe calls for moistening the dish with stock, but fresh summer tomatoes provide enough liquid.[4]

4 to 6 servings

Bread crumbs
2 to 3 large tomatoes, sliced ⅛ inch thick
Salt and pepper
2 to 3 tablespoons butter
4 to 5 eggs

Preheat the oven to 375 degrees. Pour a layer of bread crumbs into an 11 × 7-inch buttered baking dish, add a layer of sliced tomatoes, salt and pepper the slices, and repeat until the dish is full. Add another layer of bread crumbs and dot the top with butter pieces. Bake for 30 minutes total. After 20 minutes, break the eggs carefully over the top, without overlapping, and return the dish to the oven until the eggs are set, an additional 10 to 12 minutes, depending on how firm you like your eggs.

Tomatoes and Eggs

Mary M. Peter's Tomato Fricassee, 1889

We fell in love with this 1889 recipe immediately. Mary M. Peter's cookbook includes recipes credited to various women, but this one is her own. The fricassee is a rich tomato gravy, and while Mary Peter specifies serving it over toast, it would be excellent over biscuits with broiled ham for a weekend brunch.[5]

4 servings

1 (14½-ounce) can diced tomatoes
2 tablespoons butter
½ teaspoon salt
⅛ teaspoon pepper
½ teaspoon chopped onion
Pinch of baking soda
3 beaten eggs
Buttered toast

Combine the tomatoes, butter, salt, pepper, onion, and soda in a medium saucepan. Simmer for 15 minutes and add the eggs. Stir constantly and remove the mixture from the heat the moment it begins to thicken, pour it over buttered toast, and serve.

Seaton Family's Cheese Omelet, circa 1880s

While the title of this recipe suggests a traditional omelet (cooked eggs folded around some sort of filling), that is not the case for this dish. This recipe calls for pouring a milk-and-egg mixture over very thinly sliced bread and cheese and then baking it in the oven. The result, more akin to a casserole, is delicious no matter what it is called.[6]

4 to 6 servings

Tomato Fricassee

1 tablespoon butter

8 ounces shredded cheddar cheese

6 to 8 very thin slices of bread, enough to cover the bottom
    of the baking dish

¼ teaspoon salt

⅛ teaspoon cayenne pepper
⅛ teaspoon dry mustard
1 egg
1 cup milk or cream

Preheat the oven to 350 degrees. Butter an 11 × 7-inch baking dish and put a layer of cheese in it. Cover the cheese with slices of bread and add another layer of cheese. Season with the salt, cayenne pepper, and dry mustard. Mix the egg and milk and pour the mixture evenly over the bread and cheese. Bake 30 minutes or until the top begins to brown.

Louise Ludlow Dudley's Omelet with Fine Herbs, 1876

We halved the 1876 recipe, which called for 10 eggs. Honestly, we were probably just low on eggs, but it also seemed a little easier to manage a 5-egg omelet. Another option would be to divide the egg mixture and make individual omelets. The onion and parsley give this hearty omelet a great deal of flavor.[7]

2 to 3 servings

5 eggs
4 ounces cheese, grated (cheddar or mozzarella works well)
4 ounces bread crumbs
¼ cup cream or ½ cup milk
2 tablespoons finely chopped onion
1 tablespoon chopped parsley
1 teaspoon salt
⅛ teaspoon pepper
1 tablespoon butter

Beat the eggs to combine, and mix in the cheese, bread crumbs, cream, onion, parsley, salt, and pepper. Melt the butter in a skillet over medium heat. Pour in the egg mixture and cook until the bottom browns slightly. Flip the omelet and cook the other side. Fold in half and serve.

Lucy Hayes Breckinridge's Creamy Omelet, early 1900s

It seemed unlikely that a "creamy omelet" could be created using water, but this recipe did produce a fluffy and creamy omelet. Additional ingredients, such as cheese, cooked meat, or vegetables, although not in the original recipe, could be added right before the omelet is folded. Use a nonstick pan to make it easier to flip the omelet.[8]

1 to 2 servings

3 eggs
1 teaspoon melted butter
3 tablespoons water
½ teaspoon butter
½ teaspoon salt
⅛ teaspoon pepper

Beat the eggs until they are just mixed. Add the melted butter and the water. Melt the ½ teaspoon of butter in the pan and pour in the eggs. Turn the egg mixture toward the center as it becomes creamy. Season with salt and pepper and cook until it browns on the bottom. Fold the omelet in half and serve.

Lucy Hayes Breckinridge's Stuffed Eggs, early 1900s

Like the deviled eggs found at family reunions and many holiday meals in the South, these are classic in that they contain red pepper—the spice that makes them devilish. These eggs, however, don't have the famil-

Creamy Omelet and Stuffed Eggs

iar mayonnaise or relish, *but butter makes them rich and perhaps even more sinful. If you can't find onion extract, a teaspoon or more of finely chopped onion will work fine. The simple version is delicious, but the original recipe offers variations for serving—including frying.*

3 servings

3 eggs
Dash of red pepper

⅛ teaspoon salt
3 teaspoons melted butter
Few drops onion extract

Place the eggs in a saucepan of cold water and bring to a boil. Simmer for 30 minutes over medium to medium-high heat. Run cool water over the eggs and remove the shells. Let the eggs cool completely and cut them in half. Remove the yolks to a bowl and add the red pepper, salt, butter, and onion extract; combine these ingredients. Put portions of the mixture into the egg whites. The original recipe advises, "The eggs may be served thus with a plain white sauce, or put in the oven covered with breadcrumbs and white sauce, or the halves put together, dipped in breadcrumbs, diluted eggs, and breadcrumbs again, then fried."[9]

Lucy Hayes Breckinridge's Plain Foamy Omelet, early 1900s

Frothing the whites and then adding them to the yolks makes this omelet astonishingly light and fluffy. Cook in an ovenproof, nonstick pan to make it easier to remove the omelet after cooking.[10]

1 to 2 servings

3 eggs
3 tablespoons water
½ teaspoon butter
¼ teaspoon salt
⅛ teaspoon pepper

Preheat the oven to 350 degrees. Separate the eggs and beat the whites and yolks separately. Using an electric or hand mixer, take care to beat the whites until they are frothy but not stiff. Add the water to the yolks and mix. Add the beaten whites to the yolk and water mixture. Preheat an ovenproof pan, melt the butter in it, and add the egg mixture. Brown the bottom of the omelet, add the salt and pepper, and bake it until the eggs have set, 5 to 10 minutes. Fold the omelet in half and serve.

To Poach Eggs, 1881

The 1881 recipe does not call for vinegar, but the addition of 1 tablespoon or more to the poaching liquid will help the egg whites coagulate. Use a cup or small bowl to transfer the eggs gently into the water. These instructions are from the original recipe: "Have a pan boiling water; have the eggs carefully broken and slip them into the boiling water; let them remain till the whites are set, and take out with spoon; put in a dish and pour on some drawn butter."[11]

Combine roughly 8 cups of water and 1 tablespoon of vinegar in a heavy saucepan and bring it to a simmer. Break 1 egg at a time into a small bowl and slide into the water. Simmer 2 to 3 minutes or until the egg white is firm. Remove the egg with a slotted spoon onto a paper towel to dry. Repeat with other eggs.

Cooper Family's Eggs Somerset, circa 1960s

This recipe, as indicated on the typed original, was a favorite of John Sherman Cooper and his wife, the former Lorraine Arnold Rowan. Cooking the initial egg mixture requires patience to allow it to thicken properly. This dish is comfort food, pure and simple. Enjoy eggs somerset with a thick piece of toast or a biscuit.[12]

6 servings

2 cups crabmeat or lobster
1 stick butter
½ teaspoon salt

½ cup cream
Dash of cayenne pepper
Dash of paprika
Dash of nutmeg
3 eggs plus 6 eggs
3 tablespoons sherry
1 cup cream sauce (page 135)
Gruyere cheese, thinly sliced

Cook the crabmeat, butter, and salt for 3 minutes in a double boiler. Add the cream, cayenne, paprika, and nutmeg and heat thoroughly. Beat 3 of the eggs, add them, and cook until thickened. Just before removing this mixture from the heat, add the sherry. Pour the mixture into a casserole dish or, for individual servings, into 6 small pastry shells. Prepare the cream sauce. Poach the remaining 6 eggs (see the preceding recipe) and place one on top of each individual pastry shell or arrange them on top of the mixture in the casserole dish. Dot generously with the Gruyere cheese and cover with the cream sauce. Heat the broiler to 500 degrees and broil the mixture 3 to 5 minutes, or until it is brown and bubbling.

Buttering bread, circa 1940s. Louis Edward Nollau Nitrate Photographic Print Collection, University of Kentucky Libraries.

Biscuits and Breads

Good bread makes the homeliest meal acceptable, and the coarsest fare appetizing, while the most luxurious table is not even tolerable without it.

—*Esta Woods Wilcox*, Buckeye Cookery

Breads and biscuits were staples in southern cooking and an essential part of all meals. Breads were consumed at breakfast, dinner, and supper. Leftover bread was used for desserts. Bread of all kinds was made in the home, but especially corn bread was part of the rural landscape of Kentucky. As many Americans moved from the farm to cities in the twentieth century, bread increasingly became store-bought. But as these recipes show, bread-baking has a long, diverse, and delicious history. The classic Kentucky beaten biscuit could not be overlooked, and as Kentucky culinary authority Charles Patteson says, "beaten, 'doesn't mean whipped together for lightness with an egg beater or whisk; it means placed on a flat surface and pounded with a blunt instrument. . . . [Even] a tire iron will do. . . . Granny used to beat 'em with a musket.'"[1]

Lucy Hayes Breckinridge's Griddle Cakes, early 1900s

These cakes came off the griddle slightly crispy on the outside and fluffy on the inside. They do not, however, provide a lot of flavor on their own, so a topping of fresh fruit or syrup (or both) would be a welcome addition. The griddle cakes would be especially delicious topped with fresh strawberry syrup (page 130). One good feature of these griddle cakes is that they can accommodate both sweet toppings and savory ones, such as barbecue.[2]

8 griddle cakes

1 egg, separated
¾ cup water
1 tablespoon butter
1 cup flour
¼ teaspoon salt
1 teaspoon baking powder

Preheat the griddle over medium-low heat. Separate the egg white from the yolk. Combine the water and yolk together. Melt the butter and mix in; add the flour and salt and stir. When that mixture is ready, add the baking powder to the egg whites and, using an electric or hand mixer, whip until stiff. Fold the two mixtures together and drop the batter, one-fourth cup at a time, on the griddle. Cook until both sides are slightly brown.

Griddle Cakes

Louise Ludlow Dudley's Soda and Cream of Tartar Biscuits, 1876

These biscuits are a solid southern treat. Cooked as drop biscuits, they are tender and ready for butter, honey, jam, or gravy, or to be stacked with eggs and meat. The original recipe calls for lard, but butter works just fine.[3]

8 large biscuits

2 teaspoons cream of tartar
3 cups flour
1 teaspoon baking soda
6 tablespoons hot water
1 tablespoon butter, melted
Pinch of salt
About ¾ cup milk

Preheat the oven to 375 degrees. Sprinkle the cream of tartar in the flour and mix the baking soda in the hot water to dissolve it. Add the butter, salt, and baking soda with water to the flour and mix it with the milk. Drop onto a greased baking sheet and cook for 10 to 15 minutes.

Cooper Family's Beaten Biscuits, circa 1960s

Although dated 1960 in the text from the archives, this recipe probably originated much earlier. The recipe is a labor of love. Beaten biscuits are not light and fluffy; they are closer to the consistency of a thick cracker. They come from the nineteenth century, before baking powder and soda were widely available. Cooks found that if they repeatedly folded and beat biscuit dough, air pockets would form. When the biscuits baked, the heat would cause the air pockets to expand, making the biscuits rise. Traditionally, beaten biscuits are served with country ham.[4]

4 dozen small biscuits

3 cups flour
1 teaspoon salt
⅓ cup cold shortening
¾ cup cold milk

Preheat the oven to 400 degrees. Sift the flour with the salt. Cut in the shortening, add the milk, and mix until the dough becomes very stiff. Place the dough on a floured board and beat it with a rolling pin or wooden mallet for 30 minutes, folding the edges after each stroke. Roll to one-third of an inch thick and cut with a biscuit cutter or a small glass. Place the biscuits on a greased baking sheet and prick them with a fork. Bake about 20 minutes.

Frances Jewell McVey's Coffee Cake, circa 1920s

This coffee cake is nothing like the twenty-first-century store-bought variety. It is aromatic, full of spice, and moistly dense. We used a well-buttered and floured Bundt cake pan that worked nicely. You could substitute walnuts or even chocolate chips for the raisins.[5]

8 to 12 servings

1½ pounds raisins (about 4 cups)
1 pound currants (about 4 cups)
5 cups sifted flour
2⅔ sticks butter
1½ cup sugar
1 cup molasses
1 tablespoon cinnamon
1 tablespoon allspice
1 scant teaspoon cloves
1 teaspoon nutmeg

5 tablespoons bourbon
1 cup strong coffee
3 eggs, beaten
1 teaspoon baking soda

Preheat the oven to 350 degrees. Toss the raisins and currants in 2 teaspoons of the flour. Mash and cream the butter and mix in the sugar, molasses, cinnamon, allspice, cloves, and nutmeg. Add the bourbon and beat this mixture well. Dissolve the baking soda in a little of the coffee. Alternately add the flour and coffee, then the eggs beaten separately, the soda-coffee mixture, and lastly the raisin-and-currant mixture. Fill a large buttered and floured cake mold three-fourths full and bake for 50 minutes or until an inserted knife comes out clean.

Hominy Muffins

These are classic corn muffins to which hominy is added, giving the muffins a terrific moist texture. While not as well known, corn flour is a fine powder made from cornmeal. Do not use straight cornmeal in place of the corn flour, or the muffins will be too dry. If you can't find corn flour, you can pulverize the cornmeal in a food processor or coffee grinder.[6]

12 muffins

1 cup cooked hominy
1 teaspoon salt
1½ tablespoon melted butter
1 egg, beaten
¾ cup milk
2 cups corn flour
4 tablespoons baking powder

Preheat the oven to 400 degrees. Mix together the hominy, salt,

Coffee Cake

3 eggs — 1 coffee cups strong coffee
either cold or hot — 1½ cups sugar
1⅓ butter — 1 cups blackest New
Orleans molasses — 5 cups sifted
flour — 5 tablespoons whiskey —
1½ pounds (seeded) raisins —
1 pound black currents — a little
citron if desired —
1 tablespoon each cinnamon &
all-spice — 1 teaspoon nutmeg —
scant teaspoon cloves — 1 teaspoon
soda dissolved in a little of the
coffee add just before the fruit
Use coffee cups to measure.
To mix. Mix — Wash and cream
butter, add sugar molasses, then spices &
&
whiskey, beat well together, then
add alternately flour and coffee
then the eggs beaten separately, add
then soda, lastly the fruit well
floured use additional flour
for family about 2 small teaspoo
fill. Till mold ⅔ full try
with straw and so soon as it does
not stick remove from stove.

Coffee Cake

butter, egg, and milk. Sift the flour and baking powder and add them to the hominy mixture. Beat the resulting mixture well, spoon it into greased muffin tins, and bake for 20 to 30 minutes.

Spoonbread

"To be served in dish in which it is baked with spoon," says the original recipe. Perhaps we did not add enough boiling water, or maybe this is what spoonbread was like back then (although by all accounts it should have been softer). Regardless, this is quite good, whether you consider it a light corn bread or a tasty spoonbread. We used a cast-iron skillet greased with olive oil, and the spoonbread had a great crust. Cover the skillet with aluminum foil about halfway through baking to prevent the top from burning.[7]

6 to 8 servings

2 cups cornmeal
1 teaspoon salt
1 teaspoon baking soda
1 to 1½ cups boiling water
2 eggs, separated
2 cups buttermilk
1 tablespoon melted butter

Preheat the oven to 450 degrees. Grease well a cast-iron skillet and put it in the oven to heat. Sift the cornmeal, salt, and baking soda. Over them, pour enough boiling water to make a soft dough, approximately 1 to 1½ cups. Beat the egg yolks well and combine the buttermilk with them. Add the milk and yolks to the dough and stir to combine. Next, add the butter and mix well. Beat the egg whites and fold them into the batter. Pour the batter into the hot pan and bake for 35 to 40 minutes.

Hoeing the garden, circa 1916. Barker and Faulconer Fayette County Public Education photographs, University of Kentucky Libraries.

Sides

Dining in Kentucky is an art, and as an artistic expression it has been created by and, in turn, it creates the vivacity, ardor, frankness, generosity—yea even courage of the people of the Bluegrass state.

—Frances Jewell McVey

Side dishes are the support for the main dishes. In Kentucky they are diverse, as they have been for centuries in the South.

They provide contrast and typically include egg and cheese dishes, fruits, salads, vegetables, and grains. Many of the sides in Kentucky's food heritage are the vegetables grown in our gardens: potatoes, corn, carrots, onions, turnips, parsnips, tomatoes, green beans, butter beans, peas, mustard greens, kale, scallions, sweet potatoes, yellow summer squash, zucchini, cauliflower, broccoli, cucumbers, asparagus, bell peppers, cabbage, beets, and eggplant. Kentuckians also had peaches, apples, watermelons, pears, grapes, cherries, and paw paws.

Frances Jewell McVey's Crabmeat à la Newberg, circa 1920s

This recipe makes a great first course. Our contemporary version calls for claw crab meat, since lump is more expensive and would just get broken up in the sauce while cooking. The original recipe created a dish that was a little too thin, so we have added a roux for thickening. The end product is like a dip, so serve it with a sliced baguette, crackers, or something similar.[1]

2 to 4 servings

2 tablespoons butter
2 tablespoons flour
1 cup milk or cream
2 tablespoons sherry
1 egg yolk
1 (6-ounce) can claw crab meat
½ tablespoon salt
½ teaspoon black pepper
½ tablespoon paprika

Melt the butter over medium heat. Add the flour and stir to combine. Cook for 5 minutes. Add the milk and sherry, stirring to

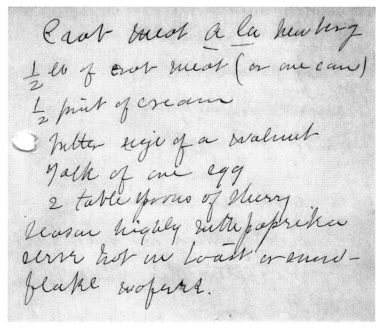

Crabmeat à la Newberg

make sure there are no lumps. Bring the mixture to just below a boil. Reduce the heat, add the egg yolk, crab meat, salt, and pepper, and simmer over low heat for 5 minutes. Pour into a bowl, top with the paprika, and serve.

Baked Hominy and Cheese

This is a creative and tasty way to cook grits. It makes enough to serve a crowd and can be reheated as a leftover. Baked hominy and cheese would be an excellent brunch or dinner side. A sharp cheddar, Swiss, or jack cheese would be best used in this dish.[2]

6 to 8 servings

3 cups water

1 cup grits
1 cup milk
1 tablespoon butter
½ tablespoon cornstarch
1 teaspoon salt
½ cup grated cheese
½ cup bread crumbs

Preheat the oven to 350 degrees. Boil 3 cups of salted water and slowly stir in the grits. Cook for 5 minutes, stirring constantly, and remove from the heat. Prepare the sauce: combine the milk, butter, cornstarch, and salt and bring the mixture to a simmer. In a small baking dish, spread half the grits and top with half the grated cheese. Add the remaining grits, then the cheese, and pour the sauce over the layers. Sprinkle the bread crumbs evenly over the top and bake uncovered for 30 minutes.

Scalloped Tomatoes, 1881

Roma tomatoes were used in this recipe, but any variety of tomato will work. This is one of those dishes that taste better when the tomatoes used are fresh and in season.[3]

6 to 8 servings

6 to 8 tomatoes (or enough to fill your baking dish)
1 clove garlic
¾ teaspoon salt
½ teaspoon black pepper
⅛ teaspoon cayenne pepper
½ tablespoon olive oil
½ cup bread crumbs (plus more to sprinkle on top before baking)

Preheat the oven to 350 degrees. Slice the tomatoes and garlic and place in a bowl. Season these ingredients with the salt, black pepper, cayenne pepper, and olive oil; mix to combine. In a baking dish alternate layers of tomatoes and bread crumbs. Sprinkle additional bread crumbs on top and bake for 30 minutes.

Josephine Funkhouser's Smothered Mushrooms, circa 1920s–1930s

These tender, rich mushrooms make an excellent starter or side for any meal, but they are especially nice when the weather turns cold. If you don't have onion juice, substitute a tablespoon of finely diced onion.[4]

4 servings

1 (8-ounce) package whole button mushrooms
1 tablespoon unsalted butter plus butter for the baking dish
¾ cup heavy cream
1 teaspoon salt
½ teaspoon pepper
1 teaspoon onion juice or 1 tablespoon onion, finely diced

Wipe the mushrooms clean with a damp towel and remove the stems. Place them in a well-buttered pan with the caps facing

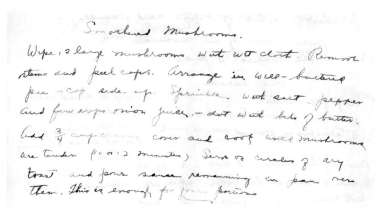

Smothered Mushrooms

up. Season them with the salt and pepper, and place a small dab of butter in each mushroom cap. Pour the onion juice over them or sprinkle them with the diced onion, add the cream, and cover and cook over medium-low heat for 10 to 12 minutes or until they are tender. Remove the mushrooms from the pan and return the sauce to a medium-low heat. Slice the mushrooms and return them to the pan for 5 minutes or until the sauce has thickened. Serve the mushrooms on toast or crackers with the sauce poured over the top.

Spurr Family's Corn Pudding, circa 1890s

A staple of southern side dishes, this corn pudding is warm and comforting. It would be excellent served alongside fried chicken.[5]

6 to 8 servings

6 ears of corn, scraped from the cob, or 2 cups frozen corn
1 teaspoon salt
⅛ teaspoon pepper
2 eggs, beaten
1 teaspoon butter

Preheat the oven to 350 degrees. Mix the corn, salt, pepper, eggs, and butter in a medium-sized baking dish and bake for 30 minutes.

Fried Eggplant, 1881

This recipe calls for soaking the eggplant in salted water, which removes the bitter taste and allows the salt to penetrate the eggplant. You will not need to salt the eggplant again before frying. This recipe would be delicious served with a simple tomato sauce or fresh basil pesto.[6]

4 to 6 servings

1 large eggplant (or 2 small)
2 eggs, well beaten
1½ cups cracker meal (crushed crackers or panko bread
    crumbs can be substituted)
⅛ teaspoon black pepper

Peel the eggplant, slice it thinly, and place the slices in salted water for 1 hour. Heat a skillet over medium heat, and add a thin layer of vegetable oil to the pan. Remove the eggplant from the salt water and pat dry. Mix the pepper with the cracker meal. Coat both sides of the eggplant slices in the egg and then the cracker meal and fry until golden brown on each side, roughly 5 minutes per side. Drain on paper towels to remove any excess oil, and serve.

Seaton Family's Parsnip Croquettes, circa 1880s

As the original recipe suggests, "this is excellent, and has been eaten by those who thought they could not eat parsnips." The original recipe calls for hot lard, but we substituted olive oil.[7]

2 to 4 servings

2 parsnips
½ tablespoon butter
½ teaspoon salt
¼ teaspoon pepper
2 tablespoons milk
Flour
Olive oil

Wash and peel the parsnips. Cut them into 2-inch pieces and place them in a pot of salted water to cover. Boil them until tender, generally 15 or 20 minutes. Drain the parsnips and mash them with the butter, salt, pepper, and milk. Put a thick layer of flour on a plate, drop a tablespoonful of the parsnip mixture on the flour, and roll it in the flour with a spoon until it is formed into a ball. Repeat this process until you have used up the parsnips.

Over medium-high heat, heat the oil in a skillet. The oil should be about ¼ inch deep in the pan. Fry until the croquettes are golden on one side and then flip. Drain them on a paper towel and serve.

Louise Ludlow Dudley's Stuffed Eggplant, 1876

This easy recipe is a great side dish in the summer when eggplant is in season. We had some concern about boiling the cut eggplant, but it really is the best way to get the flesh of the eggplant soft enough to scoop out of the skin. Panko bread crumbs were used because of their crispy texture. The original recipe calls for the eggplant slices to be topped with additional bread crumbs before they are baked, but a little Parmesan cheese sprinkled on before baking works nicely too. Top with a basic tomato sauce if desired.[8]

4 to 6 servings

2 medium eggplants
2 tablespoons butter
1 tablespoon fresh parsley
1 tablespoon fresh thyme
½ tablespoon salt
½ teaspoon black pepper
1 cup bread crumbs
1 tablespoon milk or cream
¼ cup Parmesan cheese or additional bread crumbs

Preheat the oven to 350 degrees. Bring a large pot of salted water to a boil. Halve the eggplants, leaving the stems intact, and lightly score the flesh. Cook them in the boiling water until tender, 15 to 20 minutes. Remove them from the water and let them cool until they can be handled comfortably. Scoop out the flesh, leaving the skins intact, transfer the flesh to a large bowl, and mash it well. Melt the butter in a large skillet, add the parsley and thyme, and cook for 1 minute. Add the eggplant flesh, salt, and pepper and cook for 5 minutes. Add the bread crumbs and milk and cook an additional 2 minutes. Spoon the mixture into the eggplant shells and top with the Parmesan. Place the shells on a baking sheet and bake for 15 to 20 minutes.

Louise Ludlow Dudley's Dry Hash, 1876

This dish is like the fried potatoes that your grandmother may have made. It is a low-maintenance dish that would be excellent for breakfast or brunch, or as a side for dinner. The 1876 recipe calls for "meat chopped fine"; we used bacon, but the dish would be equally good with sausage or turkey sausage, although extra oil might have to be added for the skillet phase if turkey sausage is used. The original, handwritten recipe specified no amounts, so all have been added. To enhance the flavor even further, add 1 tablespoon of fresh chopped herbs (1 teaspoon dried).[9]

4 to 6 servings

6 slices (½ pound) center cut bacon
6 medium red potatoes, cut in ¾-inch dice
½ teaspoon salt
¼ teaspoon pepper
1 tablespoon fresh chopped herbs or 1 teaspoon dried, optional

Cook the bacon in a medium-sized cast-iron skillet until crispy and set it aside to drain on a paper towel. While the bacon cooks, add the potatoes to a pot of salted water and boil for 5 minutes, until the potatoes are slightly undercooked. Drain all but one tablespoon of bacon drippings from the skillet. Crumble the bacon and mix it with the potatoes, salt, pepper, and herbs, if using. We used fresh rosemary. Place the potato mixture in the skillet and press it flat but, according to the original recipe, "do not stir it on any account." Cook it over medium heat for 30 minutes and turn the hash out onto a serving platter. The potatoes should be crispy and delicious.

Lucy Hayes Breckinridge's Potato Croquettes, early 1900s

These croquettes make a great side but are substantial enough to be served as a vegetarian entrée. One large potato makes about three large or six small croquettes. The final mixture should resemble dry mashed potatoes. If it is too dry, thin it with additional cream, added a half teaspoon at a time. If it is too wet, add some bread crumbs. Only a tiny amount of nutmeg is necessary; if too much is added, it will dominate the flavor of the croquette. We used panko bread crumbs because we like how crispy they are, but feel free to use other bread crumbs. Although not in the original recipe, sour cream and chopped fresh chives make a delicious topping for the croquettes.[10]

3 large or 6 small croquettes

1 large russet potato
2 tablespoons cream
1 tablespoon finely diced onion
½ teaspoon salt
⅛ teaspoon pepper
1/16 teaspoon nutmeg

1 egg
Bread crumbs

Peel and dice the potato, put it in a pan of salted water to cover, and bring the water to a boil. Cook the potato dice until they are fork tender, 10 to 15 minutes depending on the size of your dice. Drain them well, return them to the pan, and add the cream, onion, salt, pepper, and nutmeg. Mash this mixture as if you were making a dry mashed potato. Beat the egg well and set it aside. Cover a plate with the bread crumbs. Form the potato mixture into patties, coating them well on each side with bread crumbs; dip them in the egg and once again in the bread crumbs. Preheat a cast-iron or other skillet over medium heat and add enough vegetable oil to thoroughly coat the bottom of the skillet (there should be roughly ⅛ inch of oil in the pan). Fry the potato patties on one side until golden brown and then turn and repeat on the other side. Drain on a paper towel and serve hot.

Lucy Hayes Breckinridge's Boiled Cauliflower, early 1900s

Although we followed the directions of the original recipe and cooked the entire head of cauliflower whole, this dish can be prepared faster and more easily by cutting the cauliflower into florets first. Cooking the whole head is more dramatic as a showpiece on the table and honors the original recipe. Serve this side topped with cream sauce.[11]

1 head of cauliflower

Select a white head of cauliflower, remove any green leaves, and soak the head downward in cold water for 30 minutes (presumably to remove any insects that may be hiding in the florets; if the head is cut into pieces, the soaking would not be necessary).

Bring a pot of salted water to a boil, drain the cauliflower, and put it head down in the salted boiling water. Cook until tender, 20 to 25 minutes for the whole head or 5 to 10 minutes for florets, drain, and serve hot with cream sauce (page 135).

Logan English's Zucchini and Eggs, 1960s

This was the recipe that provided the spark of curiosity for the cookbook, but in many ways it was one of the most difficult to decipher and to come to an agreement upon. There was no mention of how to cook the eggs, for example. It was a conflict of hard-boiled versus poached. In the end we decided to poach the eggs, and the rest of the ingredients were treated as a salad to sit under the eggs.[12]

4 to 6 servings

2 zucchini, cut on the bias ¼ inch thick
2 tablespoons red wine vinegar
6 tablespoons olive oil
Salt and pepper to taste
¼ cup finely chopped parsley
2 tomatoes, cut ¼ inch thick
8 anchovy fillets
¼ cup finely chopped red onion
2 eggs, poached (page 16)

Blanch the zucchini in salted boiling water for 1 to 2 minutes. Briefly whisk the vinegar, olive oil, salt, pepper, and parsley together. Meanwhile, poach the eggs and allow them to rest until you are ready to serve. In a separate bowl, combine the tomatoes, zucchini, anchovies, and red onion and dress them with the vinegar mixture as if you were dressing a salad. Place the vegetable mixture on a platter and top it with the two poached eggs to serve.

2 eggs
2 Zuchini (cut in slight bias
　　　¾ inch
2 Tomatoes (¼ inch slices)
　　Pepper to taste
¼ cup finely chopped Red onion
8 anchovy fillets
2 Tbs red wine vinegar
¼ cup fine chopped parsley
6 Tbs. Olive oil
　　Sprinkle onion in tomato slices
　　Zuchini in boiling let simmer
　　1 or 2 minutes
Cook in quarter: garnish
fillets between eggs
Sprinkle with vinegar parsley
and oil

Zucchini and Eggs

Stuffed Tomatoes, 1897

Using ripe, summer tomatoes makes all the difference in this dish. Their flavor is accented by the fresh parsley in the stuffing to create the perfect side dish for those hot August nights. It makes a great accompaniment to fried chicken. Grating some fresh Parmesan on the tops before baking adds a nutty flavor.[13]

4 to 8 servings

    4 medium-sized ripe tomatoes
    ½ cup chopped parsley
    1 cup bread crumbs
    ½ teaspoon salt
    ¼ teaspoon pepper
    1 tablespoon olive oil

Preheat the oven to 350 degrees. Slice off the tops from the tomatoes and scoop out the insides, trying to remove as many of the seeds as possible, and discard. It is important to leave the outside of the tomato intact. In a small bowl combine the parsley, bread crumbs, salt, pepper, and olive oil and stir to combine. Stuff the tomato shells with the bread crumb mixture. Place in a shallow baking dish and bake for 30 minutes.

Scalloped Irish Potatoes

What is not to love about scalloped potatoes? They are creamy and cheesy and a real comfort food. This original recipe included no quantities or specifications for potato or cheese type. All quantities have been supplied, and they seem to have worked well, because the dish is delicious.[14]

8 to 12 servings

    3 pounds russet potatoes (roughly 6)
    2½ cups milk
    2 cups sharp cheddar cheese
    ½ tablespoon unsalted butter
    1 tablespoon salt
    ½ tablespoon black pepper

I add just a little more butter.

40

I add a little butter to each layer.

Preheat the oven to 350 degrees. Peel and thinly slice the potatoes. Heat the milk in a saucepan over medium-low heat, but do
not let it boil. Grate the cheese. Butter the bottom and sides of a
13 × 9 × 2-inch glass baking dish. Place a layer of potatoes in the
bottom, sprinkle lightly with salt and pepper, and add a thin layer
of cheese. Repeat until you reach the top of the baking dish, then
pour the hot milk over the potatoes. Add one more layer of cheese
and bake the dish for 1 hour.

Savory Potatoes

*These potatoes pair well with the tiny tenderloins of lamb recipe (page
80) because of the inclusion of the mint. This would make a tasty summer dish when mint is plentiful in the garden.[15]*

4 to 6 servings

2 to 3 large russet potatoes (enough for 2 cups diced)
⅓ cup milk
2 tablespoons butter
1 teaspoon chopped mint
1 tablespoon chopped watercress
1 teaspoon salt
Pepper to taste

Bring a large pot of salted water to a rapid boil. Peel and roughly
dice the potatoes and cook them in the boiling water until they
are fork tender, 10 to 15 minutes. Drain well. Force the potatoes
through a ricer into a bowl and add the milk, butter, mint, watercress, salt, and pepper. Beat vigorously until smooth. Check the
seasonings, reheat if needed, and serve.

Seaton Family's Seafood Salad, circa 1880s

A light, tangy, and versatile salad. The original recipe calls for breaking a lobster in two, opening the tail, extracting the meat in one piece, breaking the claws, cutting all the meat into small slices, and taking out all of the soft parts from the belly. Fortunately, there was a note that crab could be substituted, so we used a can of lump crab meat instead. We mixed in some fresh tarragon and served it as a sandwich with slices of fresh cucumber.[16]

2 servings

½ teaspoon salt
¼ teaspoon pepper
4 teaspoons vinegar (white wine vinegar is good)
4 teaspoons oil
1 (6-ounce) can lump crab meat

Mix the salt, pepper, vinegar, and oil. Add the crab meat and serve it either chilled or at room temperature. The original recipe suggests serving the salad on any kind of salad herb that you like and covering it with two hard-boiled eggs cut in slices, a few slices of cucumber, a few capers, and some fillets of anchovy. If for a dinner, ornament it with nasturtium and marigold flowers.

Josephine Funkhouser's Tomato Aspic Salad, circa 1920s–1930s

This is a creamy version of the traditional tomato aspic. It tastes fresh and light. The aspic can be chilled in a shallow glass or a baking dish or in individual ramekins.[17]

6 to 8 servings

4 green peppers
2 medium onions

1 (14½-ounce) can whole tomatoes and juice
1 teaspoon salt
2 cups mayonnaise
3 (¼-ounce) packets gelatin

Roughly chop the peppers and onions and grind them in a food processor. Add the tomatoes and grind again. If your processor is small, work in batches. Pour this mixture into a large bowl and mix thoroughly. Add the salt. Mix in the mayonnaise. Sprinkle the gelatin onto a little cool water to soften it. Make sure there is no unsoftened gelatin, and add enough boiling water to make ½ cup. Mix and stir completely into the aspic. Pour into the serving dish of your choice, cover, and chill until set.

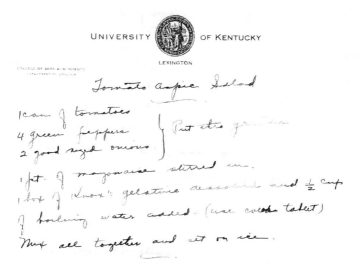

Tomato Aspic Salad

Grading corn, circa 1920s–1930s. Louis Edward Nollau F Series Photographic Print Collection University of Kentucky Libraries.

Soups and Stews

Soup is always served at dinner from palace to hovel.
—The Picayune Creole Cookbook

Soups were important staples in the American diet, especially for cooks struggling to feed their families. "For those of lesser means, soup was an important way of stretching meat, by means of grains, legumes, root vegetables, and liquid."[1] Many of these dishes could be a main course, hearty and filling, while others could be prepared as a small course in a dinner party or for a light lunch. Several of the handwritten recipes were intended to feed large groups. They were difficult to decipher and had to be scaled to make smaller quantities. One burgoo recipe, ultimately not included, would have been enough to feed ten thousand people.

Lucy Hayes Breckinridge's Corn Soup, early 1900s

Our early efforts to make this soup produced flavorful soup, but it was far too thin. A small potato was added to the soup, and it improved the texture tremendously while not taking away from the beautiful summer corn flavor. This soup can be made with frozen corn but is especially good when made with fresh, local corn. Serve the soup with croutons (page 137).[2]

3 servings as a main course, 6 as a side

1 small russet potato
6 ears of corn
3½ cups milk
1 tablespoon unsalted butter
½ tablespoon salt
½ teaspoon white pepper

Wash, peel, and dice the potato. After husking the ears of corn, remove the silk and cut the kernels from the cobs. Heat the milk in a large pot, but do not let it come to a boil. Cook the cobs in the milk for 15 minutes and discard the cobs. Simmer the kernels and the potato for 15 additional minutes or until the potato is fork tender. Puree this mixture and the butter in a food processor or

Corn Soup.

6 large or 12 small ears of corn.
1 tb. of cold water.
1 pt. of milk.
1 tbsp. of flour
1 tbsp. of butter
2 tsp. of salt
¼ tsp. of white pepper.
Small amount of onion juice.

After husking and silking corn, score and scrape.
Place cobs in a saucepan with water, boil for ten minutes,
then remove cobs and put in scraped corn. Cook ten
minutes longer. Put milk in a double boiler and cook
until hot, cream butter and flour together, mix in a
little warm milk, then pour into milk. Strain corn
into milk and add the other ingredients.
Serve with croutons.

Croutons.
Cut three half-inch thick slices of bread, remove
crust, cut into small squares, buttering the bread
beforehand, and place in oven. Cook until they
are of a golden-brown color.

Corn Soup and Croutons

blender until it is smooth. Work in batches if necessary. Strain the
mixture into a bowl, forcing as much of the liquid through the
sieve as possible. Reheat and season with the salt and pepper. Top
with croutons (page 137) and serve.

Lucy Hayes Breckinridge's Mock Bisque, early 1900s

The original recipe calls for straining the tomatoes, but this seems un-
necessary if you are using crushed tomatoes. If you would like a smoother

bisque, just puree it in a blender or use a hand mixer. Serve this soup with croutons (page 137).[3]

2 servings as a main course, 4 as a side

2 cups canned, crushed tomatoes
1 teaspoon sugar
1 bay leaf
1 tablespoon butter
1 tablespoon flour
2 cups milk
⅛ teaspoon baking soda
1 tablespoon hot water
½ teaspoon salt
¼ teaspoon white pepper

Place the tomatoes in a saucepan with the sugar and bay leaf. Bring them to a slow boil and cook for 10 minutes. Make a roux by melting the butter in a small pan and adding the flour. Stir constantly until the mixture is just barely brown. Slowly whisk in the milk and cook until the mixture is slightly thickened. Add the baking soda to the tablespoon of hot water and mix it into the tomatoes. Add the salt and pepper and stir in the milk mixture. Top with croutons and serve.

Puree of Asparagus Soup, 1897

This soup packs a lot of flavor, considering how simple it is and how few ingredients are in the recipe. To make the soup more elegant and add texture, reserve the tips of the asparagus spears after poaching to use as a garnish.[4]

3 servings as a main course, 6 as a side

2½ cups chicken stock
3 cups chopped asparagus

2 cups cream
1 teaspoon salt
¼ teaspoon pepper

Bring the chicken stock to a boil and reduce the heat. Add the chopped asparagus and simmer 10 minutes or until tender. Remove from heat and add the cream, salt, and pepper. Puree in a blender or food processor until smooth.

Frances Jewell McVey's Mushroom Soup, circa 1920s

Because the bulk of the mushrooms in this recipe are used to make a beautiful broth, the resulting soup is full of intense mushroom flavor and creates an aroma that fills the entire house. The broth is then thickened with a roux so it is creamy and thick. This incredibly simple and delicious soup would be perfect on a cool fall evening. We decided to quarter the original recipe, which made sixteen quarts of soup. We used button mushrooms, but feel free to use another variety.[5]

8 servings as a main course, 16 as a side

8 cups chicken stock
4 cups cold water
1 small onion, quartered
1 quart plus 1 cup mushrooms, cleaned
1 cup plus 2 tablespoons butter
1 cup flour
2 cups milk
2½ teaspoons salt
¾ teaspoon pepper

In a large pot combine the stock, water, onion, and 1 quart of the mushrooms, and bring them to a boil over medium-high heat. Reduce the heat and cover. Simmer over medium-low heat for 15 minutes, then turn off the heat and allow the mixture to stand for an additional 15 minutes. While this is resting, slice the additional 1 cup of mushrooms and set aside. From the stock mixture, strain out the mushrooms and onion and reserve the broth in a separate bowl. Return the pot to medium heat and melt the 1 cup of butter. Stir in the flour and allow the mixture to cook for 3 to 5 minutes to remove the raw flour flavor. Add the milk, salt, and pepper and bring it to a boil. When the mixture has thickened, add the broth and return it to a boil. Reduce the heat to low. In a sauté pan melt the 2 tablespoons of butter and cook the remaining 1 cup of thinly sliced mushrooms until they are tender. Add them to the soup and serve.

Mushroom Soup

Seaton Family's Potato Soup, circa 1880s

This soup has great flavor and texture. Although it is not in the original recipe, consider garnishing the soup with some crumbled bacon and chopped chives right before serving.[6]

4 servings as a main course, 8 as a side

4 russet potatoes
½ onion
4 cups milk
2 tablespoons butter
½ tablespoon salt
½ teaspoon black pepper

Peel and quarter the potatoes and onion, place them in a pot, and cover them with cold salted water. Bring these ingredients to a boil and cook until the potatoes are fork tender, about 20 minutes. Strain the mixture and puree the potatoes and onion with the milk in a food processor or blender. Work in batches if necessary. Return the mixture to the pot and reheat. Add the butter, salt, and pepper.

Cream of Tomato Soup

This soup can be made with fresh or canned tomatoes. If they are in season, we would recommend using fresh; they require a bit more work but give the soup an intense tomato flavor and interesting texture. Adding fresh or dried herbs such as thyme, basil, and a bay leaf also deepens the flavor of the soup.[7]

5 servings as a main course, 10 as a side

6 medium tomatoes or 1 (28-ounce) can crushed tomatoes
1¼ tablespoons salt
½ teaspoon black pepper

Pinch of cayenne pepper, optional
1 tablespoon olive oil or butter
Fresh or dried herbs, optional
2 tablespoons butter
2 tablespoons flour
2 cups milk
Pinch of baking soda

If using fresh tomatoes, bring a pot of water to a boil and fill a bowl with ice water. Score the tomatoes and place them in the boiling water for 2 minutes or until the skins begin to pull away from the flesh. Remove the tomatoes from the boiling water and shock them in the ice water to make them stop cooking. When the tomatoes are cool, peel them and remove all the seeds so that only pulp remains. Dice the tomatoes.

Place the tomatoes, salt, black pepper, cayenne pepper (if using), olive oil, and herbs (if using) in a pot and let them stew over medium heat for 20 minutes, smashing them with a wooden spoon as they stew. The more you smash the tomatoes, the smoother the soup will be. While the tomatoes are stewing, melt the butter in a saucepan over medium heat. Add the flour, stirring constantly for 1 to 2 minutes, and add the milk. Allow this mixture to warm until just below a boil. Stir the stewed tomatoes into the milk mixture, add the soda, and check the seasonings.

Lucy Hayes Breckinridge's Fish Chowder, early 1900s

This chowder is hearty, comforting, and delicious. It is hearty enough to serve as a main course. Fish stock would be ideal for this recipe, but chicken stock or water can be substituted.[8]

4 servings as a main course, 8 as a side

Fish Chowder.

2 lbs. fish.
1 pt. cold water.
1 slice of onion.
2 sq. in. salt pork.
2 potatoes.
1 cup of milk.

½ tbsp. butter.
½ tbsp. flour.
½ tsp. salt.
¼ tsp. pepper.
1 tsp. parsley
3 or 4 crackers.

Clean the fish, cut it into pieces, put in a saucepan and cover with the water. Cook twenty minutes or until the flesh separates from the bone. Cut pork into small pieces, put in frying pan, and cook until the grease has left it. Chop the onion fine, and cook until yellow in the grease. Pare and wash potatoes, cut into dice, cover with hot water, and boil five minutes. Strain water from fish, add potatoes, onion, and pork, cook until the potatoes are soft. Scald milk, cream flour and butter together, add a little hot milk and mix, add to the rest of the milk, and cook until thick. Pick the fish, removing skin and bones. Add fish and milk to water, then add the other ingredients, breaking the crackers into small pieces.

Facts about Fishes.

A fish weighing not less than two pounds may be boiled. The best fishes for boiling are bass, trout, red snapper, and rock.

If the eyes are full, the gills red, and the flesh firm, a fish is fresh.

Fish Chowder

¼ cup diced bacon or salt pork
1 small onion, finely diced
2 russet potatoes, diced
1 tablespoon salt
3 cups stock or water

1 pound white fish, such as cod or haddock, with pin bones
   removed
½ cup heavy cream
2 tablespoons chopped parsley
½ teaspoon pepper

In a 4- to 5-quart heavy pot, cook the bacon over medium heat until browned. Drain on a paper towel. Sauté the onion in the pot until it becomes translucent, 5 to 10 minutes. Add the potatoes, salt, and stock. If the potatoes are not completely covered, add more stock or water. Simmer covered for 20 to 25 minutes. While the chowder is simmering, cut the fish into 1 × 1-inch pieces. It is important to cut the pieces as uniformly as possible so that they will cook in the same amount of time. After the potatoes have cooked until they are fork-tender, use a wooden spoon or potato masher to mash some of the potatoes but not all. This will release the starch from the potatoes and help to thicken the chowder. Once the desired thickness is achieved, add the fish and heavy cream to the pot. Turn down the heat and let the fish cook for roughly 5 minutes or until white throughout. Stir in the chopped parsley and pepper carefully, so the fish does not break up, and serve.

Vegetable Soup

This soup would be a great start to a meal, and the vegetables are the star of the show. The original recipe says to "beat with spoon or fork to break vegetables." But you may leave the soup chunky or blend it until smooth to suit your taste.[9]

4 servings as a main course, 8 as a side

2 carrots
1 turnip or 2 parsnips

½ onion
1 potato
2 ribs celery
4 tablespoons unsalted butter
½ tablespoon salt
½ teaspoon pepper
½ cup chopped parsley

Peel, wash, and dice the carrots, turnip, onion, and potato. Wash and dice the celery. In a large pot over medium-low heat, melt the butter and add the carrots, turnip, and onion. Sauté for 10 minutes or until the vegetables are soft. Add the potato and sauté an additional 3 minutes. Cover with 4 cups of water, add the salt and pepper, and increase the heat to high. When the soup reaches a boil, reduce the heat and simmer 30 to 40 minutes. Finish the soup by adding the parsley and mashing or pureeing if desired.

Nannie Clay McDowell's Burgoo, 1882

There are few dishes as synonymous with Kentucky as burgoo. Many recipes call for the inclusion of meats such as squirrel, opossum, and game birds. It is a dish that was made with what was available at the time. This recipe embraces that spirit, calling for "a chicken, a piece of beef, or any meat you like." We chose to use a whole chicken, which makes a nice broth while it poaches. Interpreted literally, this is a very basic burgoo; the original recipe does not mention any seasoning whatsoever. We seasoned it simply with salt and black pepper, but garlic, Worcestershire sauce, or apple cider vinegar would add a greater depth of flavor to the final dish. The original recipe also states, "You can leave out any of the vegetables you do not like, but it is better with them all." We used frozen vegetables, but fresh can easily be substituted.[10]

8 servings as a main course, 16 servings as a side

1 (3- to 4-pound) chicken
16 cups cold water
2 tablespoons salt
1 teaspoon black pepper
7 to 10 new potatoes
1 (28-ounce) can diced tomatoes
2 cups corn
2 cups okra
2 cups peas
2 cups butter beans or lima beans
4 cups chopped cabbage

Place the chicken in a large pot, cover with the cold water, add the salt and pepper, and bring the water to a boil. Reduce the heat and allow the chicken to simmer until cooked through, roughly 1½ hours. Meanwhile, dice the potatoes. Remove the chicken and allow it to cool. Add the potatoes and tomatoes to the pot and let them simmer until the potatoes are tender, 15 to 20 minutes. Add the corn, okra, peas, beans, and cabbage and allow them to simmer an additional 15 minutes, stirring frequently. While the vegetables simmer, remove the meat from the chicken. Check the vegetables to make sure they are cooked through, and return the chicken to the pot. Add more salt and pepper to taste.

Burgon or Burgoo.   Miss Mollie Lewis'

Take a chicken, piece of beef or any
other meat you like, put it into three
gallons of water with one quart of
chopped cabbage, one pint of peas,
one pint beans, one pint of corn, one dozen
potatoes peeled & sliced, one quart of
tomatoes peeled & cored, one pint of okra
Boil five or six hours stir frequently
from the bottom or it will burn, You
can leave out any of these vegetables
that you do not like, but it is better
with them all.

Burgoo

Kentucky livestock, circa 1910–1920. Louis Edward Nollau F Series Photographic Print Collection, University of Kentucky Libraries.

Main Courses

Eating dinner in Kentucky is more than a physiological refueling of the human body, it is a joyous social ritual.
—*Thomas D. Clark,* Rivers of America

Dinner in the historic South reflected many cultural traditions and embraced meat as the main course. Meals, especially in rural landscapes such as Kentucky's, were originally driven by wild game and other local ingredients. However, pork, the first domesticated meat, has been a mainstay across the South for more than a century. The dishes in this section reflect the diversity of southern main courses in using pork, beef, seafood, game, and fowl. Sadly, we did not discover any barbecue dishes to include in this section. There are many simple main dishes here that would have utilized a leftover cut of meat, but there are just as many that could transform a contemporary dinner party.

Steak and Onions, 1910

This recipe is quick, simple, and easily adaptable to accommodate a varying number of guests. Simply plan to use a quarter of a medium onion per steak, and you can serve any number of people with this recipe. We used New York strip steaks since they are our favorite, but rib eyes or filets mignons would also work well. If your steaks are very thick, it may be necessary to finish cooking them in the oven. We have written the recipe for a single steak so that it can be easily converted to suit any number of servings.[1]

1 serving

¼ medium yellow onion
1 tablespoon butter
1 good-quality steak
1 teaspoon salt
½ teaspoon pepper
1 tablespoon vegetable oil
½ tablespoon Worcestershire sauce, optional

Slice the onion. Over medium heat preheat a sauté pan, and if the steak is particularly thick, preheat the oven to 350 degrees. Add the butter to the sauté pan and allow it melt. Season both sides of the steak with the salt and pepper. Sear it on both sides until it has a dark brown crust, about 5 minutes per side. Using a meat thermometer, check the temperature of the steak at this point;

130 to 135 degrees equals medium rare. If you prefer your steak well done, put it in the oven and check the temperature every few minutes.

Once the steak has cooked, remove it from the pan and let it rest. Return the pan to the stove, add the tablespoon of oil (if the pan is too dry) and sauté the onion over medium-low heat. When the onion starts to brown, add the Worcestershire sauce (if used) and scrape any bits off the bottom of the pan. If not using Worcestershire sauce, remove the onion from the heat when it browns. Serve the steak with the onion piled on top.

Louise Ludlow Dudley's Dish of Beef, 1876

The original recipe calls for leftover minced roast beef, but we used Kentucky ground bison instead. Feel free to use the ground meat of your choice. The recipe also calls for gravy to simmer the meat and tomatoes. Since gravy, in twenty-first-century kitchens, is not common as a pantry staple, stock was used. The mixture was allowed to simmer long enough to reduce. It is reminiscent of a shepherd's pie; a thin layer of potatoes on top will keep the flavors balanced and add texture.[2]

6 to 8 servings

14 medium or 6 small Yukon gold potatoes
1 cup milk
1 tablespoon butter
Salt and pepper to taste
1 pound ground meat, browned
1 medium onion, diced
2 cloves garlic, chopped
1½ cups chicken broth or stock
1 cup crushed tomatoes

Preheat the oven to 350 degrees. Cut the potatoes in half and then cut each half into thirds. Place the potatoes in a large pot of salted boiling water and cook them until tender, about 15 minutes. Mash the potatoes with the milk and butter and add salt and pepper to taste. While the potatoes cook, brown the meat, adding oil to the skillet if your meat is particularly lean. After the meat has browned, roughly 6 to 8 minutes, remove it. Sauté the onion in the same skillet for 8 minutes; again, add a touch of oil if the skillet gets dry. Add the garlic and sauté for 2 additional minutes. Add the broth, tomatoes, and meat; simmer for 20 minutes. Put the mixture in a baking dish, making sure it forms an even layer. Cover it with the mashed potatoes and bake for 30 minutes.

Dish of Beef

Mary M. Peter's Fillet of Beef, 1889

It is hard to believe that this recipe is from 1889. Still today it makes for a decadent main course. When the steaks have reached their desired doneness, add mushroom sauce to the pan.[3]

1 serving

1 fillet of beef
Salt and pepper
1 tablespoon butter

Preheat an ovenproof skillet over medium-high heat, and preheat the oven to 350 degrees. Season the steaks with salt and pepper. Prepare mushroom sauce (page 136) while the steaks rest. Melt the butter in the skillet and add the steaks before it begins to brown. Cook the steaks on one side until a brown crust forms, about 5 minutes. Flip the steaks and move the skillet to the oven. Cook the steaks in the oven until they reach the desired temperature, using a meat thermometer to determine doneness. The thermometer should read 130 to 135 degrees for a medium-rare steak. Pour the mushroom sauce into the skillet with the steaks and serve.

Lucy Hayes Breckinridge's Cannelon of Beef, early 1900s

The original recipe for this dish calls for chopped beef, but we found that ground beef works well as a substitute. Use lean ground round to prevent the cannelon from becoming excessively greasy. The end product is moist and pairs well with tomato sauce. Be sure to let the meat rest before slicing to keep it from drying out.[4]

4 servings

1 pound beef, chopped or ground
¼ teaspoon salt
⅛ teaspoon pepper
1 egg, well beaten
2 tablespoons melted butter
½ tablespoon finely diced onion
1 tablespoon chopped parsley

Fillet of Beef

Arrange the oven racks so that one is in the middle and another is beneath it. Preheat the oven to 425 degrees. Combine the beef, salt, pepper, egg, butter, and onion in a mixing bowl, making sure they are mixed well. Form the mixture into a log shape about 2 inches in diameter. Wrap it in greased parchment paper and twist the ends shut. Place it on the middle rack in the oven and place a pan on the rack below to catch any drippings. After 15 minutes of baking, begin basting frequently with hot water to keep the parchment from burning. Bake for 15 minutes more, remove it from the oven, and allow it to rest for 10 minutes to let the juices redistribute. Serve the cannelon with tomato sauce (page 134) and garnish it with the chopped parsley.

Cannelon of Beef and Tomato Sauce

Louise Ludlow Dudley's Fried Chicken, 1876

This is best made (and really must be made) in a cast-iron skillet with plenty of shortening. The fried chicken is incredibly crispy outside and moist on the inside. The original recipe calls for a gravy to be made from the drippings with some milk, fresh parsley, and flour if needed to thicken them. Surprisingly, this fried chicken did not seem heavy or greasy. It was delicious served with scalloped tomatoes (page 30).[5]

4 to 6 servings

4 tablespoons shortening
2 teaspoons salt
1 teaspoon pepper
1½ cups flour
6 to 8 pieces of bone-in chicken, patted very dry

Heat the shortening over medium to medium-low heat until it melts and begins to shimmer. Mix the salt, pepper, and flour in a shallow dish. Salt and pepper the chicken pieces and dredge them in the flour mixture, coating them thoroughly. Place them in a skillet and cook for 10 to 12 minutes on each side. Do not move the pieces around or turn them more than once; this will ensure that a nice crust forms and the chicken is crispy. Allow the chicken pieces to rest at least 5 minutes. They are done when they reach an internal temperature of 165 degrees or the juices run clear.

Fried Chicken

Logan English's Chicken, circa 1960s

This recipe uses some Asian ingredients to marinate the chicken. It wasn't until after World War II that condiments such as soy sauce began to be used with any frequency in the American home. The flavors of this marinade are quite strong, so it is better not to marinate overnight. The cornstarch and flour mixture forms a pleasant crispy texture, which contrasts nicely with the moist chicken inside.[6]

2 to 4 servings

¼ cup soy sauce
¼ cup honey
2 tablespoons white vinegar
1 tablespoon brown sugar
2 boneless skinless chicken breasts
4 tablespoons cornstarch
4 tablespoons flour
½ cup vegetable oil

Mix the soy sauce, honey, vinegar, and brown sugar in a baking dish or large ziplock bag. Place the chicken in the marinade, coating the chicken well. Cover the baking dish or close the ziplock bag and allow the chicken to marinate in the refrigerator for 6 hours. Bring the chicken to room temperature before cooking. Split each breast in half lengthwise. Combine the cornstarch and flour in a bowl and mix well. Put a sauté pan over medium heat and pour into it enough vegetable oil to fill the bottom of the pan. Pat the chicken dry and dredge it in the flour-cornstarch mixture. Shake off the excess. Fry the chicken in the pan for 5 to 10 minutes per side. When it is fully cooked, the thickest part of the chicken should be at 165 degrees.

Frances Jewell McVey's Chicken Pie, circa 1920s

This chicken pie, with a beautiful layer of chicken and a three-to-four-inch layer of delicious crust, looks, and tastes, like a dish that would come out of a contemporary southern gourmet restaurant. We modified the original recipe by adding vegetables. To make the pie even better, add 2 tablespoons of fresh chopped herbs to the stock before putting it in the baking dish. Any combination of thyme, rosemary, and parsley would be perfect.[7]

4 to 6 servings

Pie Filling

1 small chicken

Salt, pepper, and butter to rub chicken

3 tablespoons butter

3 tablespoons flour

3 cups chicken stock

1 carrot

1 medium-sized russet potato

1 medium onion

¼ cup frozen peas

Crust

1 teaspoon salt

8 teaspoons baking powder

2 cups flour

2 tablespoons butter

1 egg

1 cup milk

Preheat the oven to 450 degrees. In a roasting pan, rub the chicken with the salt, pepper, and butter and place it in the oven. After 20 minutes, reduce the oven temperature to 375 degrees and roast the chicken about 1 hour, or until the thickest part of the thigh registers 180 degrees.

Reduce the oven temperature to 350 degrees. In a saucepan melt the 3 tablespoons of butter over medium heat and add the flour. Stir constantly and cook for 3 to 5 minutes. Do not let this brown. Whisk in the chicken stock to avoid lumps, bring the mixture to a boil, and simmer it over low heat, stirring occasionally, just to keep it warm while you prepare and cook the vegetables. Peel the carrot and cut into ¼-inch rounds. Peel the potato and cube into ½-inch squares. Dice the onion. Bring a pot of salted water to a boil; add the potato and carrot and cook for 5 to 7 minutes. Add the onion and cook for an additional 3 to 5 minutes, until the vegetables are just tender. Drain them and add them to the stock mixture. Cut or pull the chicken into bite-sized pieces and add them to the stock mixture. Add the peas at this point and stir to combine; season with a pinch of salt and pepper. Pour everything into a small baking dish, roughly 8 × 4 inches. Shake to remove any pockets of air and smooth the top.

To make the batter: Combine the salt, baking powder, and flour. Add the butter, using a pastry blender or two knives to distribute the butter throughout the dry ingredients. Add the egg and milk and mix together. The batter will be very thin and smooth. Spread it evenly across the chicken mixture and bake for 30 minutes in the 350-degree oven.

Chicken Pie

Seaton Family's Croquettes, circa 1880s

These croquettes develop a crunchy exterior and a juicy interior. We recommend serving them with a dollop of crème fraiche, cream sauce, or a squeeze of lemon juice.[8]

8 croquettes

1 pound ground chicken or turkey
4 slices ham
1 teaspoon salt
⅛ teaspoon pepper
1 cup bread crumbs plus additional for dredging
1 teaspoon ketchup
Vegetable oil
1 egg yolk, beaten

Combine the chicken, ham, salt, pepper, 1 cup of the bread crumbs, and ketchup in a bowl until mixed well. The mixture should have the consistency of uncooked sausage. Preheat a skillet over medium-low heat and cover the bottom with vegetable oil. Form the mixture into eight patties. Dip each patty into the egg yolk, then dredge in the bread crumbs and fry on both sides until golden brown, 10 to 12 minutes per side. The patties should be firm to the touch when thoroughly cooked and register an internal temperature of 165 degrees.

Logan English's Halibut, 1960s

This is one of the more involved dishes found in the archives. It has a lot of little steps, but the end result is delicious. The flavors of the fish and vegetables meld beautifully. Use a nonstick pan for this dish to ensure that the fish will not stick while cooking.[9]

2 servings

2 medium tomatoes
1 fennel bulb
½ small onion
1 small carrot
1 clove garlic
⅛ cup olives (we used Kalamata olives)
1 anchovy fillet
1 pound halibut (swordfish or tuna could also be used)
Salt and pepper
1½ tablespoons olive oil
⅓ teaspoon dried oregano
2 tablespoons clam juice
Juice of 1 lemon
¼ cup white wine

Bring a pot of water to a boil and fill a bowl with ice water. Score the tomatoes and place into the boiling water for 2 minutes or until the skins begin to pull away from the flesh. Remove the tomatoes from the boiling water and shock them in the ice water to make them stop cooking. When the tomatoes are cool, peel them and remove all the seeds so that only pulp remains. Dice the tomatoes and reserve.

Thinly slice the fennel, onion, carrot, and garlic. Finely chop the olives and the anchovy fillet.

Heat a pan over medium-high heat. Divide the fish into two portions and season both sides with salt and pepper. Add 1 tablespoon of the olive oil to pan. When the oil starts to glisten, add the fish. Cook it 5 to 6 minutes per side so that each side develops a brown crust. Heat a sauté pan and add the remaining ½ tablespoon of olive oil and the fennel, carrot, onion, and oregano. Sauté the mixture for 5 minutes, add the garlic, and sauté an additional 3 minutes. Transfer the mixture to plates for serving. Deglaze the pan with the clam juice, lemon juice, and white wine; add the tomatoes and reduce the liquid by half. Serve the fish on top of the vegetables, pour the reduced pan sauce over all, and garnish with the olives and anchovies.

Halibut

Lucy Hayes Breckinridge's Baked Fish, early 1900s

This recipe calls for stuffing a whole fish. While that is a delicious way to prepare fish, the dish can be made with fish fillets instead. We used fillets of salmon and topped them with the stuffing, which turned crispy while baking. Finally, we topped each fillet with sauce hollandaise (page 134).[10]

4 servings

¼ cup cracker crumbs or bread crumbs
¼ teaspoon salt
⅛ teaspoon pepper
⅛ teaspoon sage
⅛ teaspoon thyme
1 teaspoon chopped parsley
4 fillets or a whole 3-pound fish, cleaned and with the eyes removed

Preheat the oven to 350 degrees. Combine in a bowl the crumbs, salt, pepper, sage, thyme, and parsley. If using a whole fish, stuff the cavity with the cracker-crumb mixture. If using fillets, rub them with olive oil and coat the top with the mixture. Place the fish on a baking sheet and bake. The whole fish will need to bake for 25 to 30 minutes. Depending on the thickness of your fillet, it should bake for 8 to 10 minutes.

Josephine Funkhouser's Salmon Croquettes, circa 1920s–1930s

These are crispy and delicious and perfect for any time of the year. You could use fresh salmon, but it is likely that Josephine Funkhouser would have used canned. According to the original recipe, if the salmon mixture is "too wet use a little cracker meal to thicken."[11]

10 to 12 croquettes

1 medium to large potato
½ teaspoon salt
3 tablespoons milk
1 tablespoon butter
1 (15-ounce) can salmon
1 egg
Approximately one sleeve of crackers

Peel and dice the potato and place it in a saucepan with water to cover. Bring it to a boil and cook until fork tender, approximately 10 minutes. Drain and return it to the pan. Add the salt, milk, and butter and mash well. Drain the salmon and break up the pieces in a medium-sized bowl. Mix in the mashed potato until well incorporated. Beat the egg in a separate bowl. Crush the crackers in a ziplock bag, using your hands or a rolling pin, until they are fine crumbs, and place them on a plate. For each croquette, make a ball using about ¼ cup of the salmon mixture. Dip the croquettes in the egg and roll them in the cracker crumbs, forming a patty shape. While forming the croquettes, heat a skillet over medium heat with enough oil to cover the bottom (about ⅛ inch deep). Fry for 5 minutes per side.

Lucy Hayes Breckinridge's Deviled Crab, early 1900s

This dish is reminiscent of classic deviled eggs with its tartness and creaminess. It could easily be served as either an appetizer or a main course.[12]

2 servings

½ cup milk
1 egg yolk

1 tablespoon flour
2 tablespoons chopped dill pickle
1 tablespoon chopped parsley
1 tablespoon butter
½ teaspoon salt
⅛ teaspoon black pepper
4 ounces crab
1 tablespoon oil
Bread crumbs
Pinch of red pepper

Preheat the oven to 350 degrees. Place the milk in a saucepan over medium heat and bring to a simmer. Whisk in the egg yolk and flour. Remove the pan from the heat and add the pickle, parsley, butter, salt, and pepper. Combine well and then mix in the crab meat and oil. Divide the mixture between two baking dishes, cover each with bread crumbs, and sprinkle with red pepper. Bake for 30 minutes.

Lucy Hayes Breckinridge's Fried Oysters, early 1900s

Written next to this recipe in Lucy Hayes Breckinridge's recipe book was the word "excellent"—a perfect description. By dipping the oysters in the bread crumbs twice, you get an incredibly crispy exterior. When you bite into these fried oysters, you get that crunch followed by the creamy interior of the oyster. These are simple, delicious, and a southern staple.[13]

2 to 3 servings

Vegetable oil, enough to half-fill the pot being used
2 tablespoons oyster liquor
⅓ teaspoon salt
¼ teaspoon pepper

2 cups bread crumbs
1 egg
1 dozen fresh oysters

Heat the oil over medium heat. Combine the oyster liquor, salt, pepper, and bread crumbs in a bowl and mix well. Beat the egg lightly in a separate bowl. Run cold water over the oysters and pat them dry. Roll the oysters in the bread crumbs, dip them in the egg, and then roll them again in the bread crumbs. The temperature of the oil should be about 375 degrees. When frying the oysters, make sure not to overcrowd the oil, as this will cause the temperature to drop. The oysters are done when a nice golden-brown crust forms on the outside.

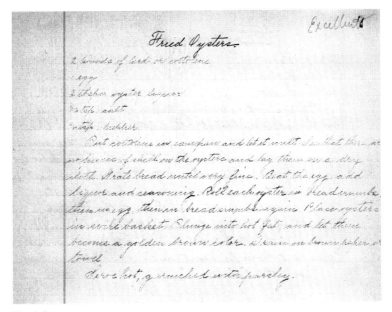

Fried Oysters

Frances Jewell McVey's Spaghetti with Celery and Ham, circa 1920s

Although it does not have the most creative name, this dish really is a delicious pasta. The long-simmered sauce develops a deep, rich flavor more intense than faster-cooking pasta sauces. This is the perfect dish to start on a Sunday afternoon for dinner that night. It also shows that southern cuisine is diverse.[14]

8 to 10 servings

1 small onion
1 carrot
2 ribs celery
3 strips bacon
1 teaspoon salt
½ teaspoon pepper
2 cups chicken stock
1 (20-ounce) can crushed tomatoes
1 pound spaghetti or other pasta
8 ounces mozzarella cheese, grated

Chop the onion, carrot, celery, and bacon into a small dice. Heat a saucepan over medium heat and add the bacon; cook until it begins to brown. Add the carrot, celery, and onion to the pan and cook until slightly brown. Add the salt, pepper, stock, and tomatoes and simmer for 40 minutes. Check the seasonings.

With 15 minutes of the 40 remaining, bring a pot of salted water to a boil and add the pasta. Cook for 7 minutes. Do not fully cook the pasta, as it will continue to cook in the oven. Preheat the oven to 350 degrees. Drain the pasta, put it in a baking dish, and pour the sauce over it. Stir to combine and cover with a layer of cheese. Bake for 40 minutes, until the top starts to brown.

Spaghetti with Celery and Ham

Cook required amount of spaghetti or macaroni in salted water and place in a buttered dish leaving plenty of room for the sauce.

Grind a small slice of ham or 2 of breakfast bacon. 2 small carrots 4 stalks of celery 2 tomatoes 1 small onion. Put all together in a saucepan with 2 tablespoons of butter and Cook until all are slightly brown, Then simmer in a pint of stock, or water in which a bullion cube is dissolved about a hour adding a little water or stock if it boils away about a pint should be left. Thicken with 2 table spoons each of butter and flour melted and rubbed together, season with salt + pepper and pour over the macaroni, combine lightly. Cover with grated cheese and brown nickly in a good oven,

Spaghetti with Celery and Ham

Mock Duck, 1910

An imitation; either this dish was meant to physically resemble another, or it was meant to taste like one. The pork loin in this recipe did not necessarily resemble duck, but it might remind one of eating duck, especially if it wasn't possible to procure a more expensive cut of meat. Whether or not the flavor of the pork in this dish is reminiscent of duck is a matter of personal taste; this main course is satisfying and delicious nonetheless.[15]

6 to 8 servings

1 pork loin, approximately 4 pounds
2 tablespoons butter
1 celery rib, diced
½ medium onion, diced
1½ tablespoons salt
¾ teaspoon black pepper
1 cup bread crumbs (or more if a larger pork loin is used)
1 tablespoon flour
2 cups water or chicken stock

Preheat the oven to 350 degrees. Split the pork loin down the middle, taking care not to cut all the way through the meat. Using a meat mallet or heavy-bottomed sauté pan, flatten the meat until it is ¼ to ½ inch thick. In a sauté pan, melt the butter and sauté the celery and onion until soft; add ½ tablespoon of the salt and ¼ teaspoon of the pepper, and then add the bread crumbs and sauté another 2 minutes. Allow the mixture to cool and spread it evenly down one side of the pork loin. Roll the loin around the stuffing in jelly-roll fashion and secure the roll with butcher's twine or toothpicks. Season the outside with the remaining 1 tablespoon of salt and the remaining ½ teaspoon of pepper. Put the loin in a roasting pan and sprinkle the flour over it. Pour over it the water and roast it for 1 hour. If the gravy is not thick enough, heat an additional 1 tablespoon of water and 1 tablespoon of flour together and whisk them into the gravy. Let the loin rest for 15 to 20 minutes, and remove the twine or toothpicks before serving.

Lucy Hayes Breckinridge's Broiled Ham, early 1900s

This ham was nicely browned on one side and remained moist. It would be a quick complement to breakfast or a country dinner. The early-twentieth-century recipe for Maître d'Hôtel butter is on page 131.

2 servings

1 slice thick ham
1 cup buttermilk

From the original recipe: "Soak a slice of ham in sour milk all night. Then wash and dry it. Cut off some of the fat and the under edge. Grease the broiler, put the ham on it with fat upwards and broil over a clear red hot fire. Put Maître d'Hôtel Butter on ham and place on shelf."[16]

Josephine Funkhouser's Tiny Tenderloins of Lamb, circa 1920s–1930s

This recipe calls for the eye of the chop to be removed, but it can be left on the bone if that is preferred. Make sure your pan is hot before adding the chops, or they will not brown. Brush the lamb chops with apple mint sauce while they are still hot so that it forms a bit of a glaze. The original document says to serve with pea puree, but no pea puree recipe was included. Andrew McGraw has supplied one.[17]

4 servings

8 lamb chops
Salt and pepper
4 tablespoons vegetable oil

Remove the "eye" of the lamb from the chops. Heat a sauté pan over medium-high heat. Season the lamb chops with a pinch of salt and pepper on each side. Add the oil to the pan and cook the chops 2 to 3 minutes per side for medium-rare doneness. Glaze the chops with apple mint sauce (page 136) and serve over pea puree.

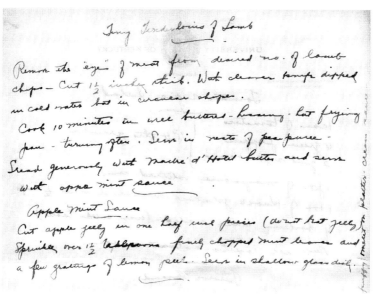

Tiny Tenderloins of Lamb

Andrew McGraw's Pea Puree

This simple side pairs well with lamb. Serve it in the spring with fresh peas, and it will be delicious. The puree can be made in the blender, although originally it was probably forced through a sieve.

4 servings

1 cup shelled peas
½ tablespoon mint
Salt and pepper to taste
1 tablespoon unsalted butter

Bring a pot of salted water to a boil. Add the peas and cook until just tender, not soft. Drain them and shock them in ice water to stop the cooking. Puree with the mint, salt, pepper, and butter.

Louise Ludlow Dudley's Roasted Partridges with Chestnuts, 1876

This recipe is perfect for serving around the holidays or whenever the weather is cold. We used jarred chestnuts; if you use fresh, make sure you boil, peel, and quarter them before adding them to the stuffing. If you cannot find partridges, substitute Cornish hens or even a small chicken. The cooking time will be greatly affected by the type of bird used.[18]

2 servings

1 sweet potato
1 teaspoon salt
¼ teaspoon pepper
¼ cup milk
1 cup quartered chestnuts
4 partridges, 2 Cornish hens, or 1 small chicken
3 to 4 strips bacon

Preheat the oven to 425 degrees. Peel and cut the sweet potato in half and then cut each half in thirds. In a large pot, boil the sweet potato until tender, about 10 to 15 minutes. Drain and mash it with the salt, pepper, milk, and chestnuts. Stuff the cavity of the birds with this mixture. Truss the legs to ensure that the stuffing does not come out during cooking. Lay the strips of bacon over the breasts of the birds. Roast them for 20 to 30 minutes or until they begin to brown, then reduce the temperature to 350 degrees to finish cooking. The internal temperature should be 165 degrees.

Decorated Cake, circa 1940s. Louis Edward Nollau Nitrate Photographic Print Collection, University of Kentucky Libraries.

Desserts

Regardless of where they lived, Southerners had a fondness for sweet desserts.

—*Susan Williams,* Food in the United States, 1820–1890

Desserts were hugely popular throughout the South in earlier years, as they continue to be today. No birthday is complete without a southern birthday cake. The availability of sugar also increased significantly in the nineteenth century as a result of the Spanish-American War, because sugar companies were allowed to import to the United States without paying a tariff. Many of the desserts in this section reflect the food trends of the time, combining "locally grown fruit, some sort of sweetener—sorghum, molasses, cane syrup, or sugar—and a flour-based pastry."[1] We have provided a single piecrust recipe, referred to as simply plain paste, which can be used for all the pies in this section. As we searched for recipes for this book, we often found that recipe collections were predominantly desserts. The bulk of the recipes we chose date from the mid- to late-nineteenth century; it is wonderful to see how they've stood the test of time.

Lucy Hayes Breckinridge's Plain Paste, early 1900s

No, this is not a recipe for glue but for an unsweetened piecrust. The recipe will make a single crust but easily doubles to make a top and bottom crust for recipes such as the one for apple pie. The original recipe calls for Cottolene, a brand of shortening made of beef tallow and cottonseed oil that was produced in the United States from 1868 until the mid-twentieth century.[2] Butter is substituted for the Cottolene in this recipe.[3]

1 piecrust

½ teaspoon salt
1½ cups pastry flour
4 tablespoons butter
¼ cup ice-cold water

Stir the salt into the flour; then cut in the butter with a pastry cutter, add the water, and mix into a crumbly paste. Roll the dough out to ½ inch in thickness, turn the ends to the center, roll out again, and repeat this process until the dough is smooth. Put it aside in a cool place.

Frances Jewell McVey's Orange Pie, circa 1920s

This pie is a surprising delight. The orange flavor is not a common choice in contemporary pies. The pie is light, refreshing, and very easy to make. It is a variation of the classic southern chess pie. Use the plain paste recipe to make a single crust or purchase a premade graham cracker crust.[4]

8 servings

Single piecrust, unbaked
½ cup sugar plus 6 tablespoons
1 tablespoon butter, softened
2 oranges
3 eggs, separated
2 tablespoons fine cornmeal

Heat the oven to 350 degrees. Prebake the crust for 3 to 5 minutes and set it aside. In a medium-sized bowl, cream the ½ cup sugar

Orange Pie

and the butter. Zest one of the oranges and squeeze both. Add the zest, egg yolks, juice, and cornmeal and mix well. Pour this mixture into the cooled crust, set it on a baking sheet, and bake for 15 minutes. While the pie is baking, make the meringue. Using an electric mixer, whip the egg whites until they are stiff. Sprinkle in the remaining sugar and whip until the meringue is smooth and shiny. Remove the pie from the oven and smooth the meringue around the edges, filling in the center last. Smooth the meringue over the top, creating a seal. Bake for an additional 15 minutes. Let the pie cool and serve it chilled.

Frances Jewell McVey's Pumpkin Pie, circa 1920s

A creamy, traditional pumpkin pie that's great for any occasion. The recipe can easily be doubled to make two. Use the plain paste recipe for the crust or a premade, purchased one.[5]

8 servings

1 egg
1½ cups pumpkin
2½ rounded tablespoons of sugar
½ teaspoon cinnamon
Pinch of nutmeg
Pinch of cloves
Pinch of allspice
1 cup milk
Single piecrust, unbaked

Preheat the oven to 350 degrees. Lightly beat the egg and add it to the pumpkin. Add the sugar, cinnamon, nutmeg, cloves, and allspice and mix well. Add the milk and stir until it is well incorporated and the mixture is smooth. Pour the filling into the piecrust and bake for 55 minutes. Let cool and serve at room temperature or chilled.

Lucy Hayes Breckinridge's Apple Pie, early 1900s

This is a simple and tart pie with very little added sugar that allows for full enjoyment of the apple flavors. The lemon juice is our addition to the original recipe. Double the plain paste recipe to make the crusts for this dessert. For a special touch, brush the top crust with an egg wash to allow the pie to brown to a golden color. To make the egg wash, simply whisk one egg with 1 tablespoon water.[6]

8 servings

4 tart apples, such as Granny Smith
Juice of 1 lemon
1 tablespoon sugar
1 teaspoon cinnamon
⅛ teaspoon freshly grated nutmeg

Preheat the oven to 350 degrees. Peel, core, and slice the apples and mix them with the lemon juice. Make 2 piecrusts (page 86). Roll the dough thin and put the lower crust in a greased pan, fit loosely to the sides. Place a layer of apples in the crust and sprinkle them with some of the sugar, cinnamon, and nutmeg. Add the remaining apples and spices in similar layers. Moisten the edge of the lower crust, put on the upper crust, and press the edges together with a fork. Make air holes in the top and bake for 25 to 30 minutes.

Parrish Family's Lemon Custard Pie, circa 1850s

This recipe makes a wonderfully creamy pie that is fast and good. The pie is not too sweet and not too tart and would be perfect served with a dollop of whipped cream. Be sure to let the pie cool completely on a wire rack before chilling. Lemon custard pie is best served after 6 to 8 hours in the refrigerator. Use the plain paste recipe or a premade piecrust.[7]

8 servings

1 piecrust, unbaked
3 eggs
1 cup milk
½ cup sugar
3 heaping tablespoons flour
1 lemon, zested and juiced

Preheat the oven to 350 degrees. Whisk the eggs in a mixing bowl and add the milk, stirring to combine. Add the sugar and flour and mix completely with a wooden spoon or whisk. Add the lemon zest and juice and mix until thoroughly combined. Pour the filling into the prepared crust and place the pie pan on a baking sheet. Bake for 40 minutes or until set in the middle. Cool, chill, and serve.

Lemon Custard Pie

Seaton Family's Sugar Pie, circa 1880s

The original recipe calls for butter the size of an egg, not an uncommon measure for recipes from this era. According to several consulted sources, that size equates to roughly three to four tablespoons of butter; however, we must admit that we formed our butter to the approximate size of an egg and measured to make sure. As is also common, no cooking times or temperatures were suggested. This pie has deep flavor from using brown sugar and just a touch of salt to balance it all out. The pie is excellent on its own, warm or chilled, and would be easily complemented with whipped cream or ice cream. Use the plain paste recipe (page 86) to make a single crust or purchase a premade graham cracker crust.[8]

8 servings

1 piecrust, unbaked
1 cup brown sugar
½ cup water
2 eggs
2 tablespoons melted butter
1 tablespoon flour
⅓ teaspoon salt

Preheat the oven to 375 degrees. Prebake the crust for 5 minutes and set aside. Add the sugar to the water in a small saucepan and bring it to a boil. Boil slowly for 5 minutes, until the mixture has slightly thickened. Beat the eggs and slowly stir in the sugar mixture to temper them. Stir in the melted butter, flour, and salt. Bake for 35 minutes.

Cocoanut Pie

This cocoanut pie (the spelling is from the original recipe) develops a lovely cream on the bottom with the coconut rising to the top. The folded egg whites brown nicely and create a delicious pie. The original recipe calls for one small coconut grated, but store-bought freshly grated coconut will work just fine. Use the plain paste recipe (page 86) to make a single crust.[9]

8 servings

1 piecrust, unbaked
4 egg yolks
1 cup sugar
1 cup unsweetened grated coconut
¼ cup coconut water
1 tablespoon lemon juice
1 teaspoon lemon zest
4 egg whites

Preheat the oven to 350 degrees. Bake the piecrust for 10 minutes. Beat the egg yolks until they are very light, add the sugar, and beat until the mixture is smooth and velvety. Mix in the coconut, coconut water, lemon juice, and lemon zest. Using an electric or hand mixer, beat the egg whites until stiff and fold them into the pie mixture. Pour the filling into the piecrust and bake for 25 minutes. Chill before serving.

Seaton Family's Carrot Pie, circa 1880s

The lemon in this tasty pie is fresh and not overpowering. While the carrots create a vivid orange color, the pie does not taste remotely like a vegetable pie. Use the plain paste recipe (page 86) or a purchased piecrust.[10]

8 servings

1 pound carrots
1 tablespoon butter
½ teaspoon salt

1 cup sugar
½ lemon, zested and juiced
3 eggs
3 cups milk
1 piecrust, unbaked

Preheat the oven to 350 degrees. Peel the carrots and cut them into rough cuts. Boil them until tender, about 10 minutes, and then strain them by rubbing through a sieve (you may use a blender, but the consistency will not be as fine). Add the butter while the carrots are still warm, then the salt, sugar, juice, and zest. Lightly beat the eggs and add them to the carrot mixture. Mix in the milk. Pour the mixture into a deep piecrust and bake for 55 minutes. Cool and chill before serving.

Spurr Family's Bourbon Pudding (Pie), circa 1890s

Our first attempt to make this bourbon pudding, although it tasted fantastic, was a failure. It was pure liquid. The original recipe has no actual cooking instructions other than to bake in a rich crust. After the initial fiasco, we realized that cooking the pudding prior to baking must have been intended in the original recipe—historically, the terms pudding and pie were often used interchangeably. We were so happy that we gave it a second chance, because this pie is sinfully rich, sweet, and divine. Use the plain paste recipe (page 86) or a purchased piecrust.[11]

8 servings

2 sticks butter
2½ cups sugar
1 cup cream
4 egg yolks, well beaten
1 tablespoon flour

Bourbon Pudding (Pie)

2 to 4 tablespoons bourbon
1 piecrust, unbaked

Preheat the oven to 375 degrees. Prebake the crust for 5 minutes and set aside. Melt the butter and sugar in a small saucepan over medium-low heat. Slowly add the cream and then the egg yolks. Mix well. Whisk in the flour until the mixture is smooth and cook until just bubbling. Stir frequently. Remove the pan from the heat and add the bourbon. Pour the filling into the piecrust and bake for 30 to 35 minutes. Let cool before serving.

Seaton Family's Cherry Tart, circa 1880s

A basic recipe but quite nice with good sour cherries—frozen will work, but be sure to use tart cherries, not Bing.

6 to 8 servings

Preheat the oven to 275 degrees. Here is the original recipe: "Have a very shallow, round tin tart mould, not more than an inch and a half deep; cover it with a thin layer of paste [plain paste, page 86]; then take some fine cherries, cut off their stems with a pair of scissors, so as not to tear the fruit—the principal beauty of a cherry tart consisting in the fruit being whole when sent to table. Pack in a single layer of the cherries, strew a good deal of sugar over them." Bake for 25 to 30 minutes.[12]

Wasan Family's Blackberry Jam Cake, circa 1835–1856

This cake is delicious because the sweetness of the jam is balanced by the spices and the tanginess of the buttermilk. It would be good any time of the year and for any occasion.[13]

10 to 12 servings

2 cups sugar
2 sticks butter
6 eggs
4 cups flour
2 to 3 cups blackberry jam
2 cups buttermilk
4 teaspoons baking soda
⅛ teaspoon allspice
⅛ teaspoon nutmeg
⅛ teaspoon cinnamon

Preheat the oven to 325 degrees. Using an electric mixer, cream the sugar and butter together until somewhat fluffy. Add the eggs and mix well. Add the flour, jam, buttermilk, baking soda, allspice, nutmeg, and cinnamon. Once combined, the mixture should make a somewhat loose batter. Pour into two buttered cake pans and bake 45 minutes to 1 hour or until a tester comes out clean. Allow to cool and serve.

Mary M. Peter's Hickory Nut Cake, 1889

This cake is so versatile. It would be delicious as a breakfast bread, a light dessert, or, iced, for something more decadent. Hickory nuts, while similar to walnuts, have a milder and richer flavor and are native to the South. To maintain the integrity of this dessert, hickory nuts were ordered. One pound of nuts, in the shell, yielded the necessary 1 cup for the cake. Shelling them was another adventure. While not entirely recommended, a good skillet and a kitchen towel work quite well. With that in mind, make sure you purchase shelled nuts.[14]

8 to 10 servings

1½ sticks butter, softened
1½ cups sugar
1¼ teaspoons baking powder

Hickory Nut Cake

2¼ cups flour
¾ cup milk
5 egg whites
1 cup hickory nut kernels

Preheat the oven to 350 degrees. Cream the butter and sugar. Whisk the baking powder into the flour. To the butter and sugar, add the milk and flour gradually. Beat this mixture until it is smooth. Beat the egg whites to a stiff froth and add them, alternating with the nuts. Pour the batter into a flat square pan and bake for 45 to 55 minutes. Cut the cake into fancy shapes, and then ice them.

Louise Ludlow Dudley's Molasses Sponge Cake, 1876

This cake has a strong molasses flavor, but that is balanced with a healthy amount of sugar. Once they are combined, they give the cake pronounced sweet and savory flavors.[15]

10 to 12 servings

2 cups sugar
1½ cups butter, softened
2 cups molasses
6 eggs
1 teaspoon vanilla
2 cups milk
6 cups flour

Preheat the oven to 450 degrees. Using an electric mixer, cream the sugar and butter until combined well. Add the molasses and add the eggs one at a time. Add the vanilla, then the milk, and add the flour one cup at a time, mixing after each addition. Pour the batter into two 9-inch cake pans and bake 40 to 45 minutes.

Frances Jewell McVey's Skillet Cake, circa 1920s

For this skillet cake, blackberries were used because they were in season and fresh at the farmer's market. Considerably less sugar was used in this version, and the result is nicely sweet without overpowering the fruit. The original recipe calls for pineapple and recommends serving the cake with whipped cream.[16]

8 to 10 servings

3 tablespoons unsalted butter
3 tablespoons brown sugar
1 stick unsalted butter, softened
1 cup sugar
2¼ cups flour
2 teaspoons baking powder
¼ teaspoon salt
4 egg whites
1 cup milk
½ teaspoon vanilla
2 cups fruit (fresh or frozen)
¼ cup toasted walnuts, optional

Preheat the oven to 400 degrees. Melt the 3 tablespoons butter and brown sugar in a 10-inch cast-iron skillet. For the cake batter, mix the ½ cup of butter and the cup of sugar with an electric mixer until light and fluffy. In a medium-sized bowl, stir together the flour, baking powder, and salt. In a small bowl, slightly beat the egg whites and stir in the milk and vanilla. To the cake-batter butter-sugar mixture, alternately add the flour mixture and the egg-milk mixture in thirds. Hand-mix until smooth. Add the fruit to the skillet and sprinkle with walnuts (if using). Pour the batter over the fruit and place the skillet on the middle rack in the

Skillet Cake

oven. Bake for 40 minutes or until an inserted toothpick comes out clean. If the top of the cake starts to brown too much, cover lightly with foil. Cool until you can handle the skillet and invert to a serving plate. This cake is best served warm with ice cream or fresh whipped cream.

Wasan Family's Cream Cake, circa 1835–1856

This cake is incredibly light in texture, similar to an angel food cake but much richer and more satisfying.[17]

10 to 12 servings

1½ cups butter
3 cups sugar
10 egg whites
2 teaspoons cream of tartar
4 cups flour
1 teaspoon baking soda
1 cup sour cream

Preheat the oven to 350 degrees. Using an electric mixer, cream the butter and sugar in a large mixing bowl. Lightly beat the egg whites and stir them into the butter mixture until it is well blended. Add the cream of tartar to the flour and sift it into the cake mixture. Stir until all of the dry ingredients are incorporated. Dissolve the baking soda in the sour cream and add the mixture to the cake batter. Mix until smooth. Divide the batter evenly between two 9-inch cake pans; tap the pans to remove any air bubbles and shake gently to even the mixture. Bake for 40 to 45 minutes. Cool the layers on a wire rack, loosen the edges, and then turn the layers out onto a rack to cool completely. Frost as desired.

Lucy Hayes Breckinridge's Sunshine Cake, early 1900s

This cake is light and delicious. Because the recipe was written on the same page as the lemon cream pudding (page 111 in this book), we de-

cided to use the pudding as a topping for the cake, and the result was spectacular.[18]

8 to 10 servings

7 eggs
1 cup sugar
1 teaspoon cream of tartar
¾ cup flour
1 teaspoon lemon extract

Preheat the oven to 350 degrees. Separate the eggs and add the sugar to the yolks. Using an electric or handheld mixer, beat the whites to stiff peaks and cut in the sugar-yolk mixture. Whisk the cream of tartar into the flour and stir those ingredients into the sugar-egg mixture. Add the lemon extract. Pour the batter into a greased pan and bake for 45 minutes. When the cake is done, turn it over and allow it to cool.

Seaton Family's Buttermilk Cake, circa 1880s

This cake is so buttery and moist that it doesn't need anything else. But, to make it extra fancy, you could pair it with chopped fresh fruit during summer months, a dusting of confectioners' sugar, or a dollop of freshly whipped cream (or all three). This recipe could easily be doubled to make a layer cake.[19]

8 to 10 servings

2 sticks butter
1 cup sugar
3 eggs
1½ cups flour
½ cup buttermilk

Preheat the oven to 350 degrees. Melt the butter and mix in the sugar. Beat the eggs. Alternately add the eggs, flour, and buttermilk to the butter-sugar mixture and mix well. Pour into a greased 9-inch cake pan and bake for 25 to 30 minutes.

Lucy Hayes Breckinridge's 1, 2, 3, 4 Cake, early 1900s

This is the cake that will be baked for every birthday for years to come. Top it with the chocolate icing recipe and you will be in heaven. We can only guess that the cake gets its name from the fact that all of the ingredients come in increments of 1, 2, 3, and 4.[20]

10 to 12 servings

1½ sticks butter
2 cups sugar
4 eggs
3 cups flour
1 cup water
1 teaspoon baking powder
2 teaspoons vanilla

Preheat the oven to 350 degrees. Using an electric mixer, cream the butter and sugar well. Separate the eggs and beat the egg yolks. Add the yolks to the butter-sugar mixture and stir until well incorporated. Add the flour and water to this mixture, alternating the two, and add the baking powder with the last of the flour. Beat the egg whites well, but not until stiff, and add with the vanilla to the batter. Grease two 9-inch cake pans, dust them with flour, and distribute the batter evenly between them. Bake for 30 minutes. Allow the cake to cool before frosting.

1, 2, 3, 4 Cake

Lucy Hayes Breckinridge's Chocolate Icing, early 1900s

This icing is unpretentious and tasty. Use it as a filling and an icing on the 1, 2, 3, 4 cake, whose original recipe it followed, and the result is magical. This icing makes you wonder why our more modern interpretation was ever invented.[21]

Enough to fill one cake; double to use as both icing and filling.

2 ounces chocolate
2 egg whites
4 tablespoons confectioners' sugar

Melt the chocolate over a double boiler. Beat the eggs to a froth and stir in the sugar and then the melted chocolate.

Mary M. Peter's Pound Cake, 1889

No mixing or baking instructions were included in this recipe, so we modeled it after other classic pound cakes. The resulting cake is dense but moist and has a strong egg flavor. The addition of a teaspoon of vanilla, brandy or other alcohol, or almond extract would balance this cake out nicely. It could be served as a breakfast bread or for an after-lunch or after-dinner treat.[22]

10 to 12 servings

2 cups sugar
2 sticks butter, softened
5 egg yolks
13 egg whites
Scant 4 cups flour

Preheat the oven to 325 degrees. Grease and flour a 10-inch tube pan. Cream the sugar and butter with an electric mixer. Mix in the egg yolks slowly, one at a time. Lightly beat the egg whites and add them alternately with the flour in stages, mixing after each addition. Pour the batter into the prepared pan and tap to level it. Bake for about 1 hour and 20 minutes, until an inserted toothpick comes out clean. Let the cake cool on a wire rack and then invert it.

Frances Jewell McVey's Bread Pudding, circa 1920s

This was one of those recipes that had to be made more than once. It was worth the extra effort because it is a classic Kentucky comfort dessert. Chocolate chips could be substituted for the raisins. We used a batard from the Bluegrass Bakery, cut into one-inch slices and left to sit on the counter to get a little stale.[23]

6 to 8 servings

5 slices of bread or equivalent
Milk
Butter for greasing
2 eggs, well beaten
1 cup sugar
2 teaspoons cinnamon
1 heaping teaspoon baking powder
About 1 cup raisins

Cover the bread with milk and let it rest for a short time. Grease a double boiler or a bowl to be used as such. Mix together the eggs, sugar, cinnamon, and baking powder. Drain the milk from the bread and put the bread in the double boiler. Pour the egg mixture over the bread. Add the raisins. Cover and cook over low heat for 1 hour.

Frances Jewell McVey's Oatmeal Cookies, circa 1920s

These cookies are excellent and easy to make. The lack of eggs and vanilla was a concern, but we lightly toasted the nuts and used a good-quality Vietnamese cinnamon, and the cookie was just as delicious and moist as those with vanilla and eggs. Toast the nuts in a dry pan over medium

Bread Pudding

Take five slices of bread or
the equivalent, Cover with water
or sweet milk and soak for
a short time, then press most of
the fluid out of the bread,
In the bread stir the yellows and
whites of two well beaten eggs
1 cup of sugar 2 teaspoon of
cinnamon ½ box of raisins and
heaping teaspoon of baking powder
Grease your double boiler and
pour into it, let cook until
done, then pour on a platter
and serve with hot sauce,
          Mrs Mulloy.

6 slices of stale bread
Crumb the bread Beat 2 eggs
2 cup sugar 1 cup butter beat very
lightly, pour over bread mixture
1 cup milk. then pour the sugar
butter mixture over the bread mixture

Bread Pudding

heat until you begin to smell them. The original recipe calls for raisins, but we substituted chocolate out of personal preference; feel free to experiment with your own choice of dried fruit or sweet morsels.[24]

4 dozen cookies

2 sticks unsalted butter, at room temperature
¾ cup sugar
½ cup milk
2½ cups flour
1 heaping teaspoon cinnamon
1½ teaspoons baking soda
1½ teaspoons baking powder
2 cups rolled or quick oats
1 cup walnuts toasted
1 cup raisins or chocolate chips

Preheat the oven to 375 degrees. Thoroughly cream the butter and sugar and stir in the milk. Add the flour, cinnamon, baking soda, and baking powder, and stir in the oats, walnuts, and raisins. Spoon 1 tablespoon of dough per cookie onto a greased baking sheet and bake for 10 to 12 minutes.

Frances Jewell McVey's Pecan Cookies, circa 1920s

This recipe makes a delicious cookie with an assertive pecan flavor. No baking times were included in the handwritten recipe.[25]

Approximately 1 dozen cookies

4 tablespoons unsalted butter
1 cup brown sugar
1 egg
¾ teaspoon vanilla extract

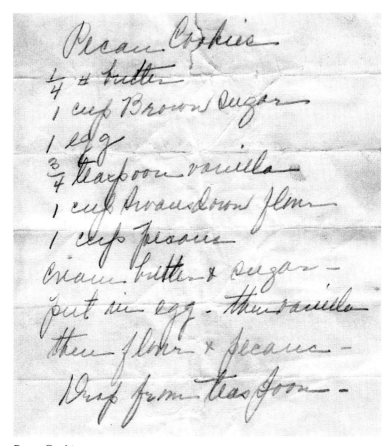

Pecan Cookies

1 cup flour
½ cup pecans

Preheat the oven to 350 degrees. Cream the butter and brown sugar; add the egg, then the vanilla, and finally the flour and pecans. Mix until well combined. Spoon onto an ungreased baking sheet and flatten lightly with the back of the spoon. Bake until the edges begin to brown, 20 to 25 minutes.

Louise Ludlow Dudley's Ginger Snaps, 1876

These ginger cookies are soft, chewy, and full of the rich flavors of ginger and molasses.[26]

Approximately 3 to 4 dozen cookies

2 sticks butter
2 cups molasses or sorghum
3 teaspoons baking soda
1 teaspoon salt
2 teaspoons ground ginger
About 2½ cups flour

Preheat the oven to 350 degrees. Mix the butter, molasses, baking soda, salt, and ginger in a saucepan and heat the mixture until it comes to a boil. Remove it from the heat. When it has cooled, add just enough flour to roll out a thin layer of the dough. Using a cookie cutter or a floured drinking glass, cut out your cookies. Bake 10 minutes on a greased baking sheet.

Frances Jewell McVey's Truffles, circa 1920s

These truffles are so simple and so wonderful. If you love chocolate, you will ask yourself why you ever purchased store-bought truffles. While the original recipe recommends rolling these in decorettes or nuts, they would be good rolled in coconut or cocoa as well.[27]

Approximately 22 truffles

8 ounces unsweetened or semisweet chocolate
1 (14-ounce) can sweetened condensed milk
1 teaspoon cinnamon
1 teaspoon butter
1 teaspoon vanilla
Crushed nuts or other coating

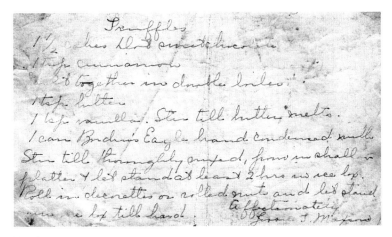

Truffles

In a double boiler, combine the chocolate, condensed milk, cinnamon, butter, and vanilla and melt the mixture, stirring until it is smooth. Cover it with plastic wrap and chill it for at least 2 hours. Roll a teaspoon of the chocolate mixture between your palms to form a ball and then roll the ball in the crushed nuts or coating of your choice. Let stand in the refrigerator until hard.

Mary M. Peter's Almond Cream, 1889

This is like a smooth version of the rice pudding that one might get in an Indian restaurant. It can be adjusted for sweetness and should be placed in its serving containers before chilling. The cream is light and simple. We ground the rice in a coffee grinder (one that is reserved for grinding spices and the like).

4 to 6 servings

4 cups milk
8 tablespoons ground rice
4 to 8 tablespoons sugar

2 to 3 teaspoons pure almond extract
Cream to serve

Boil the milk and rice until it is "as thick as mush," stirring constantly. Season it with sugar to taste and flavor with almond extract. Mold the pudding and let it chill in the refrigerator. Serve with cream.[28]

Lucy Hayes Breckinridge's Lemon Cream Pudding, early 1900s

This pudding is delicious, plain and simple. It has a loose consistency and works particularly well as a topping for cake. Try it with the sunshine cake (page 100) because the lemon flavor of the cake and pudding make them match particularly well.[29]

Topping for a single layer cake or 2 to 4 servings

4 eggs
4 tablespoons sugar
4 tablespoons water
2 tablespoons lemon juice
Zest of 1 lemon
2 tablespoons powdered sugar

Separate the eggs. Beat the egg yolks in a bowl to be used in a double boiler; add the sugar, water, lemon juice, and zest. Cook in the double boiler, stirring constantly, until the mixture has the consistency of custard. Allow it to cool for 5 minutes. Meanwhile, beat the egg whites with the powdered sugar; beat until firm but not until stiff peaks are formed. Add the pudding mixture to the egg whites, making sure to temper the whites by stirring in a small amount of the mixture first. When the pudding mixture has incorporated into the egg whites, pour the pudding into a dish and allow to cool completely.

Chocolate Filling, 1881

Use this thick filling for a sweet yellow cake or any other cake that you want to fill and top with a chocolate pudding.

Filling for one cake

1 cup sugar
2 egg yolks
2 cups milk
1 ounce (1 square) chocolate
1 teaspoon vanilla

From the original recipe: "One pint of new milk, one cup white sugar, the yolks of two eggs. Beat sugar and yolks together, then put in milk and boil until thick. Grate in one cake of sweet or Baker's chocolate and boil ten minutes. When cool flavor with vanilla. —Mrs. Joseph Mitchell."[30]

Mary M. Peter's Apricot Ice, 1889

This would be great for a summer afternoon, but it must be made a day ahead to accommodate freezing. The apricot ice is similar to a shaved ice that adults or children would enjoy. It is important to stir the mixture periodically during the freezing process as this enables the mixture to become an "ice." The recipe can easily be doubled for larger groups.[31]

Approximately 8 servings

1 (15-ounce) can apricots
4 cups water
1 cup sugar
Juice of 3 lemons

Drain the apricots (rinse if in syrup). In a medium saucepan, combine the apricots, water, and sugar. Bring these ingredients to a boil and let cook for 5 minutes. Remove them from the heat and add the lemon juice. Use a fork or potato masher to break up the apricots. Let the mixture cool and then pour it into a freezer-safe container. Stir periodically with a fork while it is freezing. Once it is solid, use a fork to scrape the mixture and form an "ice."

University of Kentucky Cosmopolitan Club, circa 1940. Cosmopolitan Club record book, University of Kentucky Libraries.

Beverages

A cup of coffee that will make any man glad he has left his mother.

—Mrs. W. T. Hayes, referring to a boiled coffee recipe in the Kentucky Cook Book

From everyday drinks like coffee, tea, and lemonade to the fancy beverages for parties or get-togethers, these recipes represent historic classic southern and regional preferences. The spice tea may not be the sweet concoction that people associate with the South, but it should become a new staple from our past. After 1865, when the first mechanical refrigeration plant for the manufacture of ice was built in New Orleans, lemonade and ice tea rose in popularity. Before drip pots or percolators came into existence, boiling coffee was the way to make the morning brew. It is definitely worth trying. The sweet and creamy dessert drinks are a carryover of the English heritage in America and are rich, strong, and delicious. The punches are strong, and the person who overindulges can choose from the several drinks that serve as restoratives, although those are fine beverages on their own.

Frances Jewell McVey's Spice Tea, circa 1920s

This drink is perfectly balanced. The orange and clove complement each other, as do the lemon and cinnamon. It's not too sweet and not too sour.

Spice Tea

We used one English breakfast black tea bag rather than loose tea. Also, if you don't want to include the fruit pulp in the tea, strain it before adding the juice to your tea.[1]

6 to 8 servings

1 tea bag
1 teaspoon whole cloves

1 stick cinnamon
½ cup sugar
Juice of 1 orange
Juice of 1 lemon

Boil 2 cups of water and steep the tea for 20 minutes. Boil another 2 cups of water and steep the cloves and cinnamon for 20 minutes. Remove the tea bag, add the sugar, and mix until it is completely dissolved. Strain out or otherwise remove the cloves and cinnamon. Combine the steeped liquids and the orange and lemon juice in a 2-quart vessel and add enough water to make 2 quarts.

Blackberry Vinegar, 1881

One has to wonder how popular temperance drinks were in Kentucky in the nineteenth century, but you do not miss the alcohol in this drink.

20 servings

4 cups berries
2 cups cider vinegar
1½ cups sugar per two cups of juice

"One gallon of fresh berries, washed and picked; pour over them half a gallon of good cider vinegar; let stand twenty-four hours; then strain. To each pint of juice add three fourths of a pound of sugar; boil half an hour, and skim carefully. When cold, bottle and cork lightly. When used, pour the depth of an inch in the glass; fill with water, pounded ice, and season with nutmeg. This is a temperance drink.—Mrs. E. McCarney."[2]

Flaxseed Lemonade, 1897

This recipe was found in the "Sick Room Cookery" section, and according to Flax: the Genus Linum, *by Alister D. Muir and Neil D.*

Westcott, flax oil has valuable fiber, lignans, and omega-3. More contemporary recipes for flax tea simplify the extraction process by boiling water and steeping flaxseeds in it for 15 minutes. However, the long simmering process in the original recipe definitely releases more from the seeds, as the resulting beverage is thicker than a conventional lemonade. Once chilled, the lemonade is tart and refreshing.[3]

2 servings

1 tablespoon whole flaxseeds
2 cups water
Juice of 2 lemons
4 tablespoons sugar

Add the flaxseeds to the water and simmer for 2 hours, but do not boil. Add the lemon juice and sugar. Chill and serve over ice.

Ginger Tea, 1839

This tea, with a great ginger flavor, would be good hot or iced. "Ginger tea is at once food and medicine. Break up some of the root ginger and boil it in clear water till just strong enough to be palatable. Then cool it and you may drink it so or sweeten it as you like. . . . It is excellent for a weak stomach."[4]

4 servings

1 (2-inch) piece of ginger
4 cups water
Sugar or honey to taste

Peel and slice the ginger into rounds. Add it to the water, bring the mixture to a boil, and simmer it for 30 minutes. Sweeten to taste.

Mint Tea, 1839

"Pick the leaves, and stalks of spare mint, rinse them clean, put them in a pitcher, and pour boiling water on, cover it, and let stand. . . . It is a sovereign efficacy in settling a sick stomach after taking an emetic."[5]

3 servings

3 cups water
3 (12-inch) sprigs of spearmint
Sugar or honey, optional

Bring the water and mint to a boil. Cover the mixture and let it stand to steep for at least 5 minutes. Remove the mint and sweeten if desired. Serve hot or cold.

Nannie Clay McDowell's Boiled Coffee, 1882

Sometimes called cowboy coffee or egg coffee, this is strong and rich. It is better than brewed coffee, but the cleanup is a labor of love for this delicious concoction. It is believed that the eggshell helps to make the grounds settle and that the alkaline properties of the egg balance out the acidic ones of the coffee, which can be bitter from the boiling. While the egg might have helped settle the grounds, straining is highly recommended before drinking.[6]

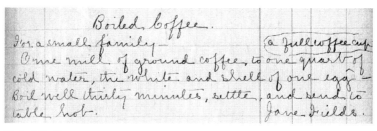

Boiled Coffee

4 to 6 servings

1 cup ground coffee
4 cups cold water
1 egg, shell and white only

Place the coffee, water, eggshell, and egg white in a saucepan and boil the mixture for 30 minutes, stirring periodically. Do not allow the coffee to boil rapidly; keep the heat at medium for a low boil. Allow the coffee to settle, and send it to the table hot.

Louise Ludlow Dudley's French Coffee, 1876

Strong, rich, and perfect for a weekend brunch. Don't even think about using milk instead of the cream.[7]

French Coffee

8 servings

1 cup ground coffee
3 cups water
1½ cup milk
½ cup cream

Brew coffee as you normally would in a pot or French press. Pour it into a saucepan with the milk and cream and heat it just to a gentle boil. Serve.

Louise Ludlow Dudley's Chocolate, 1876

The original recipe calls for two divisions of chocolate. We were uncertain of the quantity, so we started with two squares of Baker's chocolate. We both prefer our hot chocolate very rich, so we doubled the amount.[8]

6 servings

1 cup water
4 squares semisweet baking chocolate
3 cups milk

Boil the water and add the chocolate, stirring constantly until melted. Stir in the milk and bring the mixture to a slow boil. Serve.

Sarah McDowell Preston's Currant Shrub, circa 1880s

If you like a sweet cocktail, this is the one for you. The flavor of the juice is quite nice, and if you can't find black currant juice, use cranberry or pomegranate. The original recipe calls for two cups of sugar, but if you would like it less sweet, cut this amount in half.[9]

20 servings

2 cups sugar
2 cups juice
½ to 1 cup brandy

Boil the sugar and juice for 10 minutes; a light boil is best. When it is cool, add ½ to 1 cup brandy for every 2 cups of liquid. Use one part shrub to three parts ice and water.

Cooper Family's Pfirsich Bowle, circa 1960s

This is a perfect summer drink. It is cool and crisp, and peaches are perfect that time of year. If your peaches are very ripe, consider reducing the sugar. The recipe advises, "The secret to a good Bowle is to go easy on the sugar." Champagne can be used in place of soda water, and a tablespoon of brandy can be added for every cup of fruit to give this drink extra punch. The recipe does warn that if brandy is added, one should "watch out the next morning!" Try this recipe with strawberries, and you have Erdbeer Bowle. According to Lorraine Cooper, "You can use frozen or canned fruit, but I find that it never has the expected aroma and is always too sweet for my taste."[10]

16 servings

5 or 6 ripe peaches
1 tablespoon sugar for every cup of fruit
2 bottles German white wine (such as Riesling)
Soda water or champagne

Peel and slice the peaches and put them in a punch bowl. Add 1 tablespoon of sugar for every cup of fruit. Cover the fruit and sugar with half a bottle of wine, and allow this mixture to marinate overnight, covered with plastic wrap. A half hour to an hour before serving, add the remaining bottle and a half of wine to the bowl, stir, and taste for sweetness. Just before serving, add a bottle of champagne or 4 cups of soda water. Serve very cold.

Porter Soda, 1881

Soda is a lenient term for this drink. It is tart, sweet, and bitter all at the same time. Perhaps it is an acquired taste. Dissolve the tartaric acid in one cup of water; its sour taste will balance the sweetness of the sugar.

10 to 12 servings

12½ cups sugar
4 cups water
1 (22-ounce) bottle porter
4 ounces tartaric acid

"Dissolve six pounds of sugar in a quart of water, add a bottle of porter; let it simmer slowly; dissolve four ounces of tartaric acid in a tumblerful of water, stir it in just before the syrup is taken off the fire."[11]

Nannie Clay McDowell's Egg Nog, 1882

Nothing beats homemade eggnog, and in Kentucky bourbon is used instead of brandy. Other than the small substitution of bourbon for brandy in the original recipe, this is a faithful representation of the thick, strong concoction and nothing like the store-bought varieties. The original recipe states that this will make enough for a large bowl.[12]

10 to 12 servings

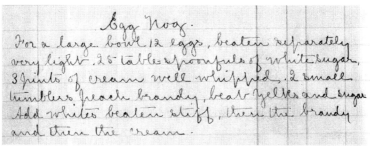

Egg Nog

12 eggs, separated
6 cups cream
1½ cups plus 1 tablespoon sugar
2 cups peach brandy

Beat the egg yolks until they are very light and the whites until they are stiff. Beat the cream until it is thick and well whipped but not stiff. Mix the egg yolks and sugar and fold in the whites. Mix in the brandy and cream. Serve well chilled.

Sarah McDowell Preston's Milk Lemonade, circa 1880s

We had serious concerns about a recipe that combines dairy and acid in one drink. Milk and lemons somehow just don't seem to go together, but in fact, they do quite nicely. This beverage was actually quite tasty and should be given a try.[13]

6 to 8 servings

2 cups boiling water
¼ cup sugar
½ cup lemon juice
¼ cup sherry
2 cups milk

Bring the water to a boil and add the sugar; stir until dissolved. Add the lemon juice and sherry and cool completely. Chill in the refrigerator and then add the milk. Serve over ice.

Mary M. Peter's Punch à la Romaine, 1889

The key to this punch is frequently stirring the lemon ice and using good dark rum. It is an excellent drink for a hot summer evening; we highly recommend it.[14]

6 to 8 servings

3 large lemons
1 cup sugar
4 cups water
2 oranges
½ to ¾ cup Jamaican rum

Zest 1 of the lemons and add the zest to the sugar and water in a saucepan. Boil for 5 minutes. Squeeze the lemons and oranges and add the juice to the pan; strain the liquid and set it aside to

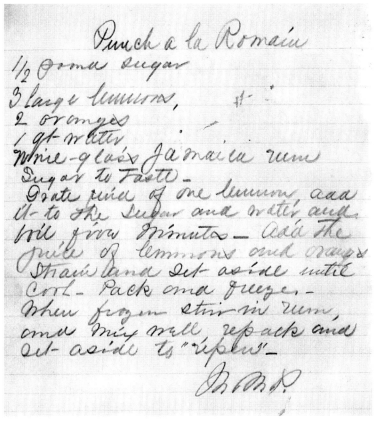

Punch à la Romaine

cool slightly. Pour it into a shallow baking dish. Once it is completely cool, place it in the freezer until it just begins to freeze. Then start stirring the mixture with a fork, to create a slushy frozen lemon ice. When it is frozen, put it into a serving container and stir in the rum. Mix the punch well and return it to the freezer until serving time.

Louise Ludlow Dudley's Punch, 1876

Strong and lemony, this punch would be refreshing on a summer day for a party. Just before serving, pour the liquid into your serving container filled with ice and lemon slices. The original recipe calls for a goblet of dark rum, which we interpreted as a cup.[15]

6 to 8 servings

4 cups brandy
1 cup dark rum, or more to taste
2 or 3 lemons
3 to 5 tablespoons sugar

Mix the brandy and rum in a sealable container. Use a vegetable peeler to remove the rind from the lemons, and add the rinds and sugar to the liquor. Let the mixture stand on the counter overnight. The next day, remove the peel and, just before serving the punch, slice the lemons and add them along with a large amount of ice. The punch needs no water but that of the melting ice.

Display of canned meats and vegetables, circa 1920s. Louis Edward Nollau F Series Photographic Print Collection, University of Kentucky Libraries.

Accompaniments

As each new vegetable or new fruit came into season, the housewife bought it in large quantities (in the city) or picked it (in the country), and threw herself into an orgy of canning.
—*Waverly Root*, Eating in America

Accompaniments include the sauces, the pickles, and the bits that might be served before or with a meal. Preserving food has a strong tradition in southern and Appalachian homes. In addi-

127

tion to putting up the vegetables or juices from the summer garden, families regularly canned jams and jellies, pickles, relishes, and sauerkraut. Meats were also preserved for later use, by salting and curing them. We found countless handwritten recipes for ketchups, pickles, relishes, chowchow, and cured meats. The challenge with most of them was that they were intended to produce large batches, using gallons of vinegar, pounds of meat, and bushels of tomatoes. The sweet bits will complement cakes, sweet breads, or griddle cakes. The cream sauces reflect a French influence and many of the dishes that southern fare is known for. And this cookbook would not be complete without a recipe for mayonnaise that has appeared in southern cookbooks since 1847.

Frances Jewell McVey's (Refrigerator) Pickles, circa 1920s

English cucumbers do not require peeling and have fewer seeds than a regular cucumber from the grocery store. If you prefer to use a regular cucumber, three small to medium-sized ones should be adequate. Unless you get them from your local farmer's market, you should peel off the waxed skin. The original recipe calls for a dozen pickles, so this recipe was scaled to make a single batch. These pickles were also too sweet for us, so the sugar was decreased to make a tarter treat.[1]

1 pint

1 tablespoon olive oil
½ cup apple cider vinegar
¼ cup sugar
½ teaspoon salt
½ tablespoon celery seed
½ tablespoon mustard seed
1 English cucumber

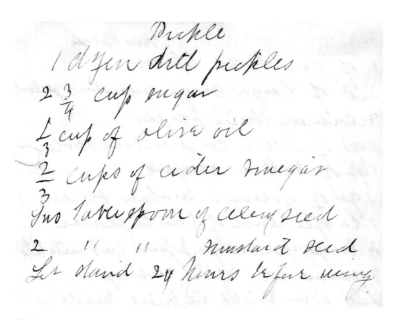

Pickle

Place the olive oil, vinegar, sugar, salt, celery seed, and mustard seed in a 1-pint mason jar and shake until these ingredients are combined. Slice the cucumber into rounds or quarter into spears and add the pieces to the jar. Gently shake the mixture to coat the cucumber pieces. Add water to cover and refrigerate for 24 hours.

Spurr Family's Ginger Nuts, circa 1890s

These nuts were a pleasant, if not an unusual, surprise. They would be good with peanuts or almonds. Peanuts would require a cooking time near the 10-minute mark, but almonds would need closer to 20 minutes. After you take them out of the oven, let them cool, and they will lose much of their stickiness. The nuts would be an interesting garnish for a salad.[2]

Approximately 4 cups

1 stick butter
4 tablespoons sugar
1 cup molasses
1 tablespoon flour
1 rounded tablespoon ginger
¼ teaspoon allspice
½ teaspoon ground cloves
½ teaspoon cinnamon
4 cups nuts

Preheat the oven to 350 degrees. Soften the butter, and cream it with the sugar. Thoroughly mix in the molasses; add the flour, ginger, allspice, cloves, and cinnamon; and mix well. Add the nuts and mix until they are evenly and well coated. Spread them on a baking sheet and bake 10 to 20 minutes.

Frances Jewell McVey's Fresh Strawberry Syrup, circa 1920s

A wonderful topping for summer pancakes or waffles. Any fresh berries could be substituted for the strawberries. We reduced the proportion of sugar to the other ingredients and found the syrup to be sweet enough. We also reduced the overall quantity to make a portion that is more manageable for a weekend brunch.[3]

Approximately 1 cup

1 cup sugar
½ cup water
1 cup cut strawberries
1 teaspoon cornstarch

Boil the sugar and water for 3 to 5 minutes. Add the berries and cook over medium heat for an additional 3 minutes. Add the

Fresh Strawberry Syrup

cornstarch and cook the mixture until the starch is gone—about 15 minutes. Strain the syrup into a storage or serving container.

Lucy Hayes Breckinridge's Maître d'Hôtel Butter, early 1900s

The original recipe calls for lemon juice, but the liquid and butter just do not mix. Zest was substituted, and the outcome was fresh and pleasant. Spread this butter on some crusty bread or use it when cooking fresh fish.

We increased the original recipe to make a larger portion, as reflected in this recipe. We served it over broiled ham (page 80) as indicated in the original recipe. Store the butter wrapped in waxed paper and freeze it for later use.[4]

8 servings

8 tablespoons unsalted butter
1 teaspoon salt
Pinch of pepper
Zest of 2 lemons
1 teaspoon lemon juice
4 tablespoons fresh flat-leaf parsley, chopped

Let the butter soften completely at room temperature. Cream it and add the salt, pepper, lemon zest and juice, and parsley. Mix thoroughly and either serve the butter right away or refrigerate or freeze it.

Nannie Clay McDowell's Mayonnaise, 1882

Mayonnaise is often referred to as one of the southern sauces, and this version is perfect. It is a fairly traditional mayonnaise, except that it contains cayenne pepper. The original recipe calls simply for vinegar, but since most contemporary recipes specify white wine vinegar, the latter was used instead. We made the mayonnaise by hand and suggest you do the same, despite the temptation to use a blender or food processor.

6 servings

2 egg yolks
1 teaspoon salt
⅛ teaspoon cayenne pepper
1 cup vegetable oil
2 tablespoons vinegar

Whisk together the egg yolks, salt, cayenne pepper, and 1 teaspoon of the oil until the mixture "appears like a cream." Slowly add the remainder of the oil while whisking to ensure that the mayonnaise does not separate. Once all of the oil has been incorporated, the mixture should have a thick custardlike consistency. Whisk in the vinegar and check the seasoning. Add more cayenne if you want it to have a nice kick.[5]

Anonymous Chile Sauce, circa 1850s

The original recipe calls for twenty-four ripe tomatoes, eight onions, six peppers, eight coffee cups of vinegar . . . and is meant to be canned. We cut the recipe to one-eighth of the original since we did not plan on canning the sauce. This sauce is quite pungent and slightly reminiscent of an Asian chili sauce. It would make a nice marinade for pork tenderloin or would serve well as a dipping sauce.[6]

16 servings

3 ripe tomatoes
1 small bell pepper
1 onion
6 ounces vinegar
1 tablespoon sugar
1 tablespoon salt
¾ teaspoon cinnamon
¾ teaspoon allspice
¾ teaspoon nutmeg
¾ teaspoon cloves

Quarter the tomatoes and remove the stems. Core and chop the pepper. Peel and roughly chop the onion. Grind the tomatoes, onion, and pepper in a food processor and pour these ingredients into a saucepan. Add the vinegar, sugar, salt, cinnamon, allspice, nutmeg, and cloves, and mix well. Bring to a boil.

Lucy Hayes Breckinridge's Tomato Sauce, early 1900s

This recipe pairs perfectly with cannelon of beef (page 63). It has a subtle spice flavor from the inclusion of cloves.[7]

Approximately 1 cup

1 tablespoon whole cloves
1 (¼-inch) slice of onion
½ (14½-ounce) can diced tomatoes
1 tablespoon butter
1 tablespoon flour
¼ teaspoon salt
⅛ teaspoon pepper
1 tablespoon chopped parsley

Insert the cloves into the slice of onion. Put the tomatoes in a saucepan over medium-low heat and add the studded onion slice. Boil the mixture for 10 minutes and strain the juice, pressing firmly on the tomato pulp to make sure you get all the juice. In another pan, brown the butter over medium heat, being careful not to let it burn. Add the flour and cook, stirring frequently, until the mixture is brown. Add the juice, stirring constantly, and season with the salt and pepper. Before serving, check the seasoning to see if more salt or pepper is required. Garnish with the chopped parsley.

Lucy Hayes Breckinridge's Sauce Hollandaise, early 1900s

This is not a traditional hollandaise sauce that would be found in a French cookbook. But the incorporation of a roux makes it much more likely that the sauce will not break. It is still rich and delicious and con-

tains considerably less butter than a standard hollandaise, which means you can use as much as you like![8]

3 to 4 servings

> 1 tablespoon butter
> 1 tablespoon flour
> 1 cup water
> ¼ tablespoon salt
> ⅛ tablespoon pepper
> 1 egg yolk
> ½ lemon, juiced (about 1 to 1½ tablespoons)

Melt the butter in a saucepan. Stir in the flour and cook 1 to 2 minutes to remove the raw flour flavor. Add the water and bring to a boil. When the mixture thickens, remove it from the heat for 1 to 2 minutes until it cools slightly and stir in the salt, pepper, egg yolk, and lemon juice.

Lucy Hayes Breckinridge's Cream Sauce, early 1900s

This is a very basic white sauce, consisting of a roux with milk and seasonings. It pairs well with boiled cauliflower (page 37) but could be used any time you would like to add extra richness to a dish.[9]

3 to 4 servings

> 1 tablespoon butter
> 1 tablespoon flour
> 1 cup milk
> ¼ teaspoon salt
> ⅛ teaspoon white pepper

Melt the butter in a saucepan. Stir in the flour and cook 1 to 2 minutes; do not allow the mixture to brown. Stir the milk in slowly and then the salt and pepper. The sauce will not reach full thickness until it comes to a boil.

Josephine Funkhouser's Apple Mint Sauce, circa 1920s–1930s

What this recipe produces is more of a glaze than a sauce. Serve it by basting it on roasted or grilled meat, fish, or vegetables. For a perfect pairing, use this sauce on tenderloins of lamb (page 80).[10]

4 servings

2½ tablespoons apple jelly or apple butter
1½ tablespoons mint, finely chopped
1 teaspoon lemon zest

Combine the jelly, mint, and zest in a bowl and mix well.

Mary M. Peter's Mushroom Sauce, 1889

Button mushrooms would work fine in this sauce, but for a more interesting flavor, experiment with different varieties. Be sure to bring the milk to a boil slowly so that it does not scald, but it must reach a boil for the butter and flour mixture to fully thicken the sauce. Serve over Mary M. Peter's Fillet of Beef (page 62).[11]

4 to 6 servings

8 ounces mushrooms
1 stick butter, softened
4 cups milk
3 tablespoons flour
Salt and pepper

In a sauté pan, cook the mushrooms until tender over medium heat with 1 tablespoon of the butter and a pinch of salt and pepper. In another pan, over medium-low heat, slowly bring the milk to a

Mushroom Sauce

gentle boil. Rub the remaining butter and the flour into a smooth paste, and when the milk reaches a boil, whisk in the butter-flour mixture. Reduce the heat, season with salt and pepper, add the mushrooms, and serve. You may also keep the sauce warm over low heat until ready to serve.

Lucy Hayes Breckinridge's Croutons, early 1900s

Homemade croutons are economical, are better than store-bought varieties, and are the perfect use for leftover stale bread.[12]

Approximately 27 croutons

3 slices stale bread, ½ inch thick
Butter

Preheat the oven to 350 degrees. Remove the crust from the slices of bread, spread them with butter, and cut them into small squares. Bake them until they are golden brown, approximately 10 to 12 minutes.

Acknowledgments

Our foremost thanks go to the individuals who captured these recipes and passed them down to their family members, and to those who ultimately donated them to the University of Kentucky Libraries Special Collections. In addition to the women and men who collected the recipes and the cookbooks containing some of them, we acknowledge the household employees who in many cases cooked these dishes. They are the unnamed champions.

There is no way to know whether these recipes were made by the women and men who collected them. We know that many of the families would have had African American cooks who prepared their meals. In the introduction to the 2005 edition of *The Blue Grass Cook Book*, Toni Tipton-Martin describes the African Americans as a generation of invisible cooks. There still may be undiscovered collections of African American family recipes within the University of Kentucky Libraries Special Collections, but for this cookbook early American culture and domestic relations remain intertwined in a complicated way. The relationship between white women and their black cooks is a dimension of the history of southern food and culture that has shaped current culinary tastes. We hope this book will inspire further research into this important area of American history.

Many individuals contributed to this project. We appreciate all of our tasters: Brigitte Abernathy, Greg Abernathy, Tracy Campbell, Henry Huffines, Carol McGraw, Marcus McGraw,

Acknowledgments

Dean McMahan, Matthew McMahan, Helen Morrison, Neil Morrison, Rebekah Reeves, Matt Ritchie, Alison Scaggs, Carla Scaggs, Marilyn Scaggs, Roger Scaggs, Dave Wachter, and Shanna Wilbur. Thanks also to the Special Collections staff and neighborhood partygoers who were unwitting participants in the successful completion of this project.

There are a few people who washed more than one dish: Carla Scaggs, Rebekah Reeves, and Shanna Wilbur. Deirdre doesn't have an automatic dishwasher, but Andrew did—until this project rendered it useless. We are grateful also to the dedicated readers who helped us fine-tune the manuscript: Carol McGraw, John van Willigen, Marcus McGraw, Rebekah Reeves, and Shanna Wilbur.

Without all of the failed recipes, this project would not have been a success, so we would like to thank the following recipes for making us stronger: White Mountain Cake (the first recipe attempted and horribly failed), Molasses Pie, Vinegar Pie, Apple Fritters, Scalloped Oysters, Butterscotch Pie, Seven Minute Frosting, and Macaroni. A lesson we learned in the process is that you have never really bonded with someone until you have taken turns strenuously beating dough for biscuits for thirty minutes—especially when you mess it up and have to do it all over again.

The many local purveyors must be acknowledged as well: Good Foods Co-op, the Lexington Farmers Market, Weisenberger Mills, and all the local farmers. Resources that we frequently consulted include early American cookbooks, the *Joy of Cooking*, the *Oxford Companion to Food*, and our kitchen conversion chart.

We would also like to thank the dean of University of Kentucky Libraries, Terry Birdwhistell, along with all of our friends, family members, colleagues, student assistants, and peers for their support and encouragement throughout this process. We thank the University of Kentucky Libraries for preserving these amazing resources and for allowing use of the photographs and the handwritten recipes.

Notes

Egg and Cheese Dishes

1. Frances Jewell McVey papers, University of Kentucky Libraries.
2. *Modern Recipes: Dishes De Luxe by the Presbyterian Church (Lexington, Ky.) Pastor's Aid Society,* undated.
3. *Modern Recipes.*
4. Frances Jewell McVey papers, University of Kentucky Libraries.
5. E. I. "Buddy" Thompson papers, University of Kentucky Libraries.
6. Seaton family papers, University of Kentucky Libraries.
7. Scott D. Breckinridge, Jr. Collection, University of Kentucky Libraries.
8. Scott D. Breckinridge, Jr. Collection, University of Kentucky Libraries.
9. Scott D. Breckinridge, Jr. Collection, University of Kentucky Libraries.
10. Scott D. Breckinridge, Jr. Collection, University of Kentucky Libraries.
11. *Housekeeping in the Bluegrass: A New and Practical Cookbook,* ed. Ladies of the Presbyterian Church in Paris, Kentucky (Cincinnati: Robert Clarke, 1881).
12. John Sherman Cooper Collection, University of Kentucky Libraries.

Biscuits and Breads

1. R. Gerald Alvey, *Kentucky Bluegrass Country* (Jackson: University Press of Mississippi, 1992), 261.

2. Scott D. Breckinridge, Jr. Collection, University of Kentucky Libraries.

3. Scott D. Breckinridge, Jr. Collection, University of Kentucky Libraries.

4. John Sherman Cooper Collection, University of Kentucky Libraries.

5. Frances Jewell McVey papers, University of Kentucky Libraries.

6. *Modern Recipes: Dishes De Luxe by the Presbyterian Church (Lexington, Ky.) Pastor's Aid Society,* undated.

7. *Modern Recipes.*

Sides

1. Frances Jewell McVey papers, University of Kentucky Libraries.

2. *Modern Recipes: Dishes DeLuxe by the Presbyterian Church (Lexington, Ky.) Pastor's Aid Society,* undated.

3. *Housekeeping in the Bluegrass: A New and Practical Cookbook,* ed. Ladies of the Presbyterian Church in Paris, Kentucky (Cincinnati: Robert Clarke, 1881).

4. William D. Funkhouser papers, University of Kentucky Libraries.

5. Richard Alexander Spurr papers, University of Kentucky Libraries.

6. *Housekeeping in the Bluegrass.*

7. Seaton family papers, University of Kentucky Libraries.

8. Scott D. Breckinridge, Jr. Collection, University of Kentucky Libraries.

9. Scott D. Breckinridge, Jr. Collection, University of Kentucky Libraries.

10. Scott D. Breckinridge, Jr. Collection, University of Kentucky Libraries.

11. Scott D. Breckinridge, Jr. Collection, University of Kentucky Libraries.

12. English family papers, University of Kentucky Libraries.

13. Jennie Benedict, *A Choice Collection of Tested Receipts with a Chapter on Preparation of Food for the Sick* (Louisville: J. P. Morton, 1897).

14. *Modern Recipes.*

15. *Modern Recipes.*

16. Seaton family papers, University of Kentucky Libraries.

17. William D. Funkhouser papers, University of Kentucky Libraries.

Soups and Stews

1. Susan Williams, *Food in the United States, 1820s–1890* (Westport, CT: Greenwood Press, 2006) 25.

2. Scott D. Breckinridge, Jr. Collection, University of Kentucky Libraries.

3. Scott D. Breckinridge, Jr. Collection, University of Kentucky Libraries.

4. Jennie Benedict, *A Choice Collection of Tested Receipts with a Chapter on Preparation of Food for the Sick* (Louisville: J. P. Morton, 1897).

5. Frances Jewell McVey papers, University of Kentucky Libraries.

6. Seaton family papers, University of Kentucky Libraries.

7. *Modern Recipes: Dishes De Luxe by the Presbyterian Church (Lexington, Ky.) Pastor's Aid Society,* undated.

8. Scott D. Breckinridge, Jr. Collection, University of Kentucky Libraries.

9. *Modern Recipes.*

10. The Henry Clay Memorial Foundation papers, University of Kentucky Libraries.

Main Courses

1. Lina Dunlap, *Out of the Blue Grass: A Book of Recipes* (Lexington, KY: Press of Transylvania Print, 1910).

2. Scott D. Breckinridge, Jr. Collection, University of Kentucky Libraries.

3. E. I. "Buddy" Thompson papers, University of Kentucky Libraries.

4. Scott D. Breckinridge, Jr. Collection, University of Kentucky Libraries.

5. Scott D. Breckinridge, Jr. Collection, University of Kentucky Libraries.

6. English family papers, University of Kentucky Libraries.

7. Frances Jewell McVey papers, University of Kentucky Libraries.

8. Seaton family papers, University of Kentucky Libraries.

9. English family papers, University of Kentucky Libraries.

10. Scott D. Breckinridge, Jr. Collection, University of Kentucky Libraries.

11. William D. Funkhouser papers, University of Kentucky Libraries.

12. Scott D. Breckinridge, Jr. Collection, University of Kentucky Libraries.

13. Scott D. Breckinridge, Jr. Collection, University of Kentucky Libraries.

14. Frances Jewell McVey papers, University of Kentucky Libraries.

15. Dunlap, *Out of the Blue Grass.*

16. Scott D. Breckinridge, Jr. Collection, University of Kentucky Libraries.

17. William D. Funkhouser papers, University of Kentucky Libraries.

18. Scott D. Breckinridge, Jr. Collection, University of Kentucky Libraries.

Desserts

1. Susan Williams, *Food in the United States, 1820–1890* (Westport, CT: Greenwood Press, 2006), 131.

2. Alice Ross. "Cottolene and the Mysterious Disappearance of Lard." *Journal of Antiques and Collectibles,* February 2002. http://www.journalofantiques.com/Feb02/hearthfeb.htm.

3. Scott D. Breckinridge, Jr. Collection, University of Kentucky Libraries.

4. Frances Jewell McVey papers, University of Kentucky Libraries.

5. Frances Jewell McVey papers, University of Kentucky Libraries.

6. Scott D. Breckinridge, Jr. Collection, University of Kentucky Libraries.

7. Parrish family papers, University of Kentucky Libraries.

8. Seaton family papers, University of Kentucky Libraries.

9. *Modern Recipes: Dishes De Luxe by the Presbyterian Church (Lex-*

ington, Ky.) Pastor's Aid Society, undated.

10. Seaton family papers, University of Kentucky Libraries.

11. Richard Alexander Spurr papers, University of Kentucky Libraries.

12. Seaton family papers, University of Kentucky Libraries.

13. Hart family papers, University of Kentucky Libraries.

14. E. I. "Buddy" Thompson papers, University of Kentucky Libraries.

15. Scott D. Breckinridge, Jr. Collection, University of Kentucky Libraries.

16. Frances Jewell McVey papers, University of Kentucky Libraries.

17. Hart family papers, University of Kentucky Libraries.

18. Scott D. Breckinridge, Jr. Collection, University of Kentucky Libraries.

19. Seaton family papers, University of Kentucky Libraries.

20. Scott D. Breckinridge, Jr. Collection, University of Kentucky Libraries.

21. Scott D. Breckinridge, Jr. Collection, University of Kentucky Libraries.

22. E. I. "Buddy" Thompson papers, University of Kentucky Libraries.

23. Frances Jewell McVey papers, University of Kentucky Libraries.

24. Frances Jewell McVey papers, University of Kentucky Libraries.

25. Frances Jewell McVey papers, University of Kentucky Libraries.

26. Scott D. Breckinridge, Jr. Collection, University of Kentucky Libraries.

27. Frances Jewell McVey papers, University of Kentucky Libraries.

28. E. I. "Buddy" Thompson papers, University of Kentucky Libraries.

29. Scott D. Breckinridge, Jr. Collection, University of Kentucky Libraries.

30. *Housekeeping in the Bluegrass: A New and Practical Cookbook,* ed. Ladies of the Presbyterian Church in Paris, Kentucky (Cincinnati: Robert Clarke, 1881).

31. E. I. "Buddy" Thompson papers, University of Kentucky Libraries.

Beverages

1. Frances Jewell McVey papers, University of Kentucky Libraries.
2. *Housekeeping in the Bluegrass: A New and Practical Cookbook,* ed. Ladies of the Presbyterian Church in Paris, Kentucky (Cincinnati: Robert Clarke, 1881), 143.
3. Jennie Benedict, *A Choice Collection of Tested Receipts with a Chapter on Preparation of Food for the Sick* (Louisville: J. P. Morton, 1897), 79.
4. Lettice Bryan, *The Kentucky Housewife: Containing Nearly Thirteen Hundred Full Receipts, and Many More Comprised in Other Similar Receipts* (Cincinnati: Shepard and Stearns, 1839), 424.
5. Lettice, *The Kentucky Housewife,* 424.
6. The Henry Clay Memorial Foundation papers, University of Kentucky Libraries.
7. Scott D. Breckinridge, Jr. Collection, University of Kentucky Libraries.
8. Scott D. Breckinridge, Jr. Collection, University of Kentucky Libraries.
9. Preston-Johnston family papers, University of Kentucky Libraries.
10. John Sherman Cooper Collection, University of Kentucky Libraries.
11. *Housekeeping in the Bluegrass.*
12. The Henry Clay Memorial Foundation papers, University of Kentucky Libraries.
13. Preston-Johnston family papers, University of Kentucky Libraries.
14. E. I. "Buddy" Thompson papers, University of Kentucky Libraries.
15. Scott D. Breckinridge, Jr. Collection, University of Kentucky Libraries.

Accompaniments

1. Frances Jewell McVey papers, University of Kentucky Libraries.
2. Richard Alexander Spurr papers, University of Kentucky Libraries.

3. Frances Jewell McVey papers, University of Kentucky Libraries.

4. Scott D. Breckinridge, Jr. Collection, University of Kentucky Libraries.

5. The Henry Clay Memorial Foundation papers, University of Kentucky Libraries.

6. E. I. "Buddy" Thompson papers, University of Kentucky Libraries.

7. Scott D. Breckinridge, Jr. Collection, University of Kentucky Libraries.

8. Scott D. Breckinridge, Jr. Collection, University of Kentucky Libraries.

9. Scott D. Breckinridge, Jr. Collection, University of Kentucky Libraries.

10. William D. Funkhouser papers, University of Kentucky Libraries.

11. E. I. "Buddy" Thompson papers, University of Kentucky Libraries.

12. Scott D. Breckinridge, Jr. Collection, University of Kentucky Libraries.

Selected Resources

Archival Materials, all from the University of Kentucky Libraries Special Collections

Scott D. Breckinridge, Jr. Collection, 1801–2000

The Breckinridge family papers contain materials pertaining to Scott Dudley Breckinridge Jr. and his family. The Family Series documents Scott Breckinridge's relatives: primarily the Breckinridges, but also the Baynes and other families. It also contains some genealogical information as well as papers pertaining to individual family members. There are a few original documents from the nineteenth and early twentieth centuries, and there is a significant amount of correspondence about family history.

Within the Family Series are the recipe books of Louise Ludlow Breckinridge and her daughter Lucy Hayes Breckinridge. Louise's recipe book begins in May 1876 and provides some of the earliest dated recipes included in this cookbook. Louise Ludlow Dudley was born in Lexington in 1849. She was the daughter of Ethelbert Ludlow Dudley (1818–1862), a prominent Kentucky physician and a member of the faculty at the Transylvania Medical School. In 1866 Louise married Joseph Cabell Breckinridge Sr., a member of the prominent bluegrass Breckinridge family. He was a major in the Union army under William Tecumseh Sherman and later became a general in the U.S. Army; he also served as inspector general for the army. Louise and Joseph Breckinridge had at least thirteen children, including Lucy Hayes

Breckinridge. The recipes from this collection are fairly extensive and are exquisitely handwritten in bound journals.

The Henry Clay Memorial Foundation Papers, 1777–1991

The Henry Clay Memorial Foundation papers contain papers from the Clay, McDowell, and Bullock families and a few operating records for the foundation. Organized into series by family, the papers include various forms of documentation, such as correspondence, letter books, diaries, checks, receipts, account books, ledgers, stud books, drawings, paintings, printed materials, realia, and newspaper clippings.

There are many recipes in the Anne "Nannie" Clay McDowell subseries, which is part of the McDowell family papers. Henry Clay's granddaughter Anne Clay McDowell was born February 14, 1837, to Henry Clay Jr. and Julia Prather. Anne married Henry Clay McDowell in 1857. During the Civil War, her two brothers fought on opposing sides: Henry Hart for the Union and Thomas Julian for the Confederacy. Both brothers died of fevers in 1862 and 1863. Following the end of the war, Anne lived at Woodlake farm and later at her grandfather's estate, Ashland, with her family and her unmarried sister-in-law Magdalen, who worked as an artist. After Henry Clay McDowell died in 1899, Anne continued to live at Ashland until her death in 1917. The specific recipe book used for this project is handwritten, signed by Nannie Clay McDowell, and dated February 14, 1882.

John Sherman Cooper Collection, 1927–1972

The Cooper Collection includes the personal and political papers of John Sherman Cooper, U.S. senator from Kentucky. Each of the twelve main series contains personal, political, and general papers within one or more subject files. The recipes in this collection are in a folder marked as such and are typed, some on U.S. Senate letterhead.

English Family Papers, 1884–1986

The English family papers contain works created by Frederick W. Eberhardt, Logan B. English, and Logan E. English. The collection primarily consists of the personal papers, works, and writings of Logan Eberhardt English, a poet, folksinger, actor, and playwright from Bourbon County, Kentucky.

Logan E. English was born in Paris, Kentucky, November 29, 1928, to Corilla Eberhardt English, an opera singer before marriage, and Dr. Logan B. English, a Baptist minister, farmer, and prominent civic activist. Logan (the son) was raised at Wyndhurst, a historic mansion on the site of their family farm in Bourbon County. He graduated from Millersburg Military Institute and earned a bachelor's degree at Georgetown College in 1951, majoring in speech and English. After a brief period in the army during the Korean War, Logan E. English entered the Yale School of Drama in 1953, earning a master of fine arts degree in 1956.

His career as a folksinger and songwriter began professionally after his move to New York City in 1956. He made a total of six albums, comprising primarily Kentucky folk ballads, reprises of Woody Guthrie's songs, and children's folk classics. He toured extensively across the United States and in Canada, performing on college campuses, at Carnegie Hall, and at the World's Fair in New York.

The recipes from the Logan English papers were found in several notebooks that were filled with handwritten poems, songs, and even notes on wine. These sophisticated recipes show that Logan English had a passion for food and cooking; he even turned a recipe into a poem. Many of these main courses involve old and unfamiliar cooking techniques. But by and large they are simple comfort food, the sort of dishes best enjoyed with family and friends.

William D. Funkhouser Papers, 1881–1948

The Funkhouser papers include William D. Funkhouser's Zoology Department records at the University of Kentucky as well as logs of trips, scrapbooks, newspaper clippings, and other volumes. In addition to documenting Professor Funkhouser's career, his collection contains a series regarding the papers of his wife, Josephine Kinney Funkhouser.

Josephine H. Kinney was born December 7, 1881, in Pennsylvania and studied at Cornell University. In the 1910 United States census, Josephine was living with her aunt in Ithaca, New York, and was listed as a teacher. During this period, William Funkhouser was a lodger at the same residence and listed as an instructor at a high school. According to the *Kentucky Encyclopedia*, the two married on June 29, 1910.

The Josephine Funkhouser papers consist of correspondence and files on gardening, home repairs, decorating, and cooking. There is a small collection of recipes, all handwritten, many of them on University of Kentucky letterhead.

Hart Family Papers, 1787–1919

The Hart family papers document the Hart and Wasan families. Dr. R. S. Hart practiced medicine in the community of Pisgah in Woodford County, Kentucky. In addition to Dr. Hart's daybooks and account books, one volume describes cattle and hog pedigrees. The Wasan family material, dated 1835–1856, contains medical case histories and directions for making simple medical remedies. The Wasan family material is where the recipe book is located, and some individual recipes are attributed to Wasan family members. The handwritten journal is quite deteriorated, but the handwriting is neat; many of the recipes are attributed to other individuals.

Frances Jewell McVey Papers, 1857–1953

The Frances Jewell McVey papers include McVey's personal and professional correspondence, manuscripts and research notes, diaries, address books, notebooks, documents, recipes, photographs, and scrapbooks. These materials span most of the years of McVey's life, from 1889 to 1945, and document her childhood through adulthood.

Frances Jewell was born December 23, 1889, to Asa and Elizabeth Jewell in Harrison County, Kentucky. When she was a small child, the family moved to Lexington, where Frances graduated from Sayre College before going to the Baldwin School in Bryn Mawr, Pennsylvania. She received her bachelor of arts from Vassar College in 1913 and a master of arts degree from Columbia University in 1918. She was awarded an honorary doctor of laws degree from the University of Kentucky in 1940.

Frances Jewell held several positions at the University of Kentucky, beginning as a professor in the English Department from 1915 to 1921, then as the dean of women from 1921 to 1923. In 1923 she married Frank LeRond McVey, then president of the university, and was highly regarded for her role as the "First Lady of Maxwell Place." The McVeys were the first president's family to reside in Maxwell Place, and Frances was widely praised for her graciousness as hostess of many teas and dinners. Her interest in and recipes for traditional Kentucky and other southern foods were well known and publicized, as was her knowledge of gardening. Her papers contain an extensive collection of handwritten recipes for her entertaining at Maxwell Place.

Parrish Family Papers, 1825–1889

The Parrish family papers include mainly account books and breeding books. The majority of the unbound material consists of receipts issued to Dabney W. Parrish. The volumes are account books that include expenditures of money, notes of places visited, Civil War battles, amounts of hemp broken, and breeding records. Also present are separate stock breeding records, recipes for cooking foods, medical formulas, and household hints.

The Parrish family lived in the central Kentucky area in the mid-nineteenth century. Among these personal and business papers are handwritten recipes in a bound journal. The handwriting is quite legible.

Preston-Johnston Family Papers, 1755–1962

The Preston-Johnston family papers reflect the personal and professional lives of several generations of family in Kentucky. The family papers include correspondence, diaries, diplomas and certificates, wills, school records, business papers and financial transaction records, photographs, genealogical charts, and a variety of mementos from members of the family. General Preston married Margaret Wickliffe, and in 1883 their son, Robert Wickliffe Preston, married Sarah Brant McDowell, granddaughter of Virginia governor and congressman James McDowell. The Sarah McDowell Preston series contains correspondence, financial documents, diaries, address books, cards, programs, and recipes. In addition there are Daughters of the American Revolution documents, Women's Club of Central Kentucky documents, Women's Social and Political Union literature, and other miscellaneous materials. The recipes, a small collection, are handwritten on loose pages and are dated around the 1800s.

Seaton Family Papers, 1788–1956

The Seaton family papers include both personal and business-related correspondence, financial records, legal documents, memorabilia, newspaper clippings, journals, scrapbooks, and photographs. The collection relates primarily to the Means family of Ashland, Kentucky, who played a dominant role in the development of the iron industry in the Hanging Fork region of southern Ohio and in eastern Kentucky. The Means were also prominent in the development of both river and rail transportation in the area and in the formation of Ashland, Kentucky, as an industrial city.

The Seaton and Means families were joined when William Biggs Seaton married Eliza Isabella Means in 1885. The collection contains a scrapbook that may have belonged to Harriet Hildreth Perkins Means (1826–1895), the wife of John Means (1821–1910). The scrapbook of recipes is densely packed with old clippings documenting a wide spectrum of recipes. A few handwritten recipes are included.

Spurr Family Papers, 1844–1960, 1878–1899 (bulk dates)

The Richard Alexander Spurr papers contain financial records, genealogical sketches, autograph albums, photographs, recipe books, clippings, and materials relating to the United Daughters of the Confederacy. During the Civil War, Richard Alexander Spurr served under Confederate general John Hunt Morgan. At war's end, he returned to his farm in Fayette County, Kentucky.

The majority of the papers consist of family correspondence between R. A. Spurr and his brother Marcus A. of Nashville, Tennessee; Spurr's wife, Ruth Sheffer Spurr; and their children: Julia Hughes, Laura Sheffer, and Richard Hughes. Also included is correspondence with Laura's husband, Carl Welsh, of Lexington, Kentucky. The handwritten recipes are in a bound journal and are quite difficult to read; the journal is found in the materials pertaining to Laura Sheffer.

E. I. "Buddy" Thompson Papers, 1800–1940

The "Buddy" Thompson collection contains documents pertaining to Lexington history. Elmer Thompson was born in Maysville, Kentucky, in 1920 and moved to Lexington as a young boy. He married Mildred "Peg" Thompson and they had one son, Joseph Clay Thompson. In 1964 Thompson, along with James L. "Jim" Riley, established the Thompson & Riley Auction and Realty Company. Through his business, Thompson acquired many items pertaining to Lexington history, several of which are included in his papers. Thompson retired in 1982. Thompson is best known for his book *Madame Belle Brezing*, published in 1983, in which he describes the life of the Lexington prostitute Belle Brezing, who was thought to inspire the character Belle Watling in *Gone with the Wind*.

The Mary M. Peter 1889 cookbook is located within the Marion Ross series. According to the 1900 U.S. Census, Mary McCauley was born in December 1851 or 1859. She married Alfred M. Peter in 1889, the year her handwritten cookbook is dated. The 1925 certificate of Mary M. Peter's death lists her parents as John McCauley and Mary Coleman. Alfred and Mary resided at 268 E. Maxwell St. in Lexington. Alfred was a chemist at the Experiment Station at the Agricultural and Mechanical College of Kentucky (later named the University of Kentucky). Mary was a homemaker. According to the *Kentucky Encyclopedia*, Alfred M. Peter's father, Dr. Robert Peter, was responsible for bringing photography to the Commonwealth of Kentucky.

Perhaps Mary's cookbook was compiled during a time when she had increased responsibilities in the kitchen or a greater desire to be of service to her family or to be creative in this respect. We may never know the reasons; however, we are able to surmise from her recipes that they were collected from others and that every one that was tested was impeccable. Her cookbook has several other recipe contributors, whose names are indicated in handwriting that is often too difficult to read. In this cookbook we have not attempted to attribute recipes to these contributors.

Cookbooks, all from the University of Kentucky Libraries Special Collections

Benedict, Jennie. *A Choice Collection of Tested Receipts with a Chapter on Preparation of Food for the Sick.* Louisville: J. P. Morton, 1897.

Bryan, Lettice. *The Kentucky Housewife: Containing Nearly Thirteen Hundred Full Receipts, and Many More Comprised in Other Similar Receipts.* Cincinnati: Shepard and Stearns, 1839.

Dunlap, Lina. *Out of the Blue Grass: A Book of Recipes.* Lexington, KY: Press of Transylvania Print, 1910.

Housekeeping in the Bluegrass: A New and Practical Cookbook. Edited by the Ladies of the Presbyterian Church in Paris, Kentucky. Cincinnati: Robert Clarke, 1881.

Modern Recipes: Dishes De Luxe by the Presbyterian Church (Lexington, Ky.) Pastor's Aid Society. Undated.

Index

CPSIA information can be obtained at www.ICGtesting.com
Printed in the USA
BVOW07*0948251113

337106BV00002B/7/P